BATS

Look for these and other books in the
Lucent Endangered Animals and Habitats Series:

The Amazon Rain Forest
The Bald Eagle
The Bear
Birds of Prey
The Condor
The Cougar
Coral Reefs
The Crocodile
Dolphins and Porpoises
The Elephant
The Giant Panda
The Gorilla
The Jaguar
The Manatee
The Oceans
The Orangutan
The Rhinoceros
Seals and Sea Lions
The Shark
Snakes
The Tiger
Turtles and Tortoises
The Whale
The Wolf

Other related titles in the Lucent Overview Series:

Endangered Species
Energy Alternatives
Garbage
The Greenhouse Effect
Hazardous Waste
Oil Spills
Ozone
Population
Saving the American Wilderness

BATS

BY VICTORIA SHERROW

Endangered
Animals &
Habitats

LUCENT BOOKS, INC.
SAN DIEGO, CALIFORNIA

Library of Congress Cataloging-in-Publication Data

Sherrow, Victoria
    Bats / by Victoria Sherrow.
        p. cm. — (Endangered animals & habitats)
    Includes bibliographical references and index (p.   ).
Summary: Discusses these helpful flying mammals, their enemies,
loss of habitat, rescue efforts, and their future.
    ISBN 1-56006-728-4 (hardback)
    1. Bats—Juvenile literature. 2. Endangered species—Juvenile liter-
ature. [1. Bats. 2. Endangered species.] I. Title. II. Series.
QL737.C5 S52 2001
599.4—dc21

                                               00-012368

Contents

Introduction

THE SIGHT OF bats crossing the nighttime sky, their scalloped wings silhouetted against the moon, used to send people scurrying into their homes. These odd-looking animals were both feared and disliked in most parts of the world. However, many people now welcome bats, knowing that they eat insects and other pests and do not normally pose a threat to humans.

Although for centuries bats were among the least-studied animals on the earth, interest in bats has been growing since the 1970s. Scientists have studied bat physiology and the behavior of different species. New instruments enable people to study bats in the wild, as well as in captivity, and to keep track of their movements, feeding habits, reproductive patterns, and life spans. Researchers have found more ways to locate these creatures who are nocturnal—that is, active after dark. As a result, we have learned much about bats and their vital contributions to the balance of nature and to the economy.

Bats around the world

There are more than 925 different kinds of bats, and they are found all over the world except at the North and South Poles. Bats can survive in cold climates, damp climates, and dry climates, although the largest bat colonies are found in temperate regions. They live on every continent except Antarctica, and on oceanic islands and archipelagoes.

Because bats are mainly tropical animals, species are most numerous around the equator. They are most diverse in

South and Central America, where there are about twice as many species of bats as in parts of Africa, Asia, and Australia, which share similar climates.

Of all mammalian species, an astonishingly high proportion—about 25 percent—are bats, and in the tropics, bats make up about 50 percent of the mammalian species. On some islands, they are the only native mammals. Worldwide, bats have the second highest number of species, after rodents, the order of animals that includes mice, rats, squirrels, chipmunks, and rabbits.

Emerging from a cave, hundreds of bats are silhouetted against the early evening sky.

Endangered or Threatened?

Environmental agencies and organizations classify plants and animals in the wild as *endangered, threatened*, or *sensitive*. *Endangered* means that a species is seriously threatened with extinction throughout all or a significant portion of its range. *Threatened* means that a species is likely to become endangered throughout a significant portion of its range if threats to its survival are not removed within the foreseeable future. *Sensitive* means that a species is vulnerable or declining, though not threatened at this time; it is likely to become threatened or endangered if threats are not removed. By giving a species protected status, agencies obtain support for their work to remove such threats as habitat loss. Sometimes, the designation *species of special concern* is used to mean that numbers are declining and special management is needed to prevent further losses.

Declining numbers

Bat populations have declined greatly since the 1950s. Numerous species of bats are endangered or threatened, and more than a dozen species may already be extinct. According to the U.S. Fish and Wildlife Service, around 40 to 50 percent of bats in the United States are considered endangered. Six of the forty-five species that live in the continental United States are on the federal list of endangered species. Three more species that live in the state of Hawaii and in U.S. territories are also endangered. Twenty other species are considered at risk.

Indiana bats are one example of an endangered species. Despite their name, these bats live in several different states. They were among the first bats to be placed on the U.S. Fish and Wildlife Service's list of endangered species. At one time millions of Indiana bats inhabited North America. According to an endangered species specialist for the service, they numbered about 800,000 in 1973, but by 1998 the estimated population had declined to some 350,000.

Threats to bats

The main threat to bats is the loss of their habitats and food sources due to a growing human population. This results in increased environmental pollution as well as deforestation—that is, the cutting down of trees—not only to use as fuel and building materials but also to clear the land for urban, industrial, or agricultural development.

Other human activities, such as pest control programs, cave exploration, and the destruction of old mines result in many bat deaths each year. In some cases, people deliberately kill large groups of bats. They regard these bats as dangerous carriers of disease or as threats to their crops or livestock. Large colonies of bats in caves have been viciously destroyed by vandals armed with sticks, stones, or guns. Bats also die when exposed to unfamiliar predators, which happens, for example, when their habitats are destroyed and they are forced to relocate to new areas.

Working to save bats

Around the world, governments, organizations, and individuals are working to save more bat species from extinction. The number of bat conservationists has grown dramatically since the 1970s. People are working in numerous ways to protect bats and their habitats and roosting places. They educate the public about bats and their important roles as pest eaters and propagators of key plants and trees. Conservation organizations help people to safely remove bats from homes and other places where they are not wanted. They promote wooden bat-house kits and urge people to construct these artificial roosting sites to attract bats to their property.

The media are also describing bats in more positive ways. Articles, books, and programs about bats appear regularly. Photographers have captured images that show bats clinging to smiling humans, looking timid, gentle, and likable. Photos taken before the 1980s usually showed bats baring their teeth and appearing to threaten the person behind the camera.

Young people are also much more informed about bats. Nonfiction books and articles give them facts about these fascinating mammals and show them the important roles bats play in the environment. Likewise, some fiction books feature appealing bat characters. An illustrated children's book called *Stellaluna*, by Janell Cannon, attracted fans of all ages when it was published in 1993. It is a fictitious account of the adventures of a young fruit bat. To go with the book, there is a stuffed bat with wings that velcro together so that Stellaluna can hang upside down. Other toy bats and bat model kits are also being sold for young people.

Through protective laws, public education, and rescue programs, conservationists are making an impact, but many

A nineteenth-century drawing of a girl riding a gentle bat. Positive images of bats, such as this, were rare until the modern media began portraying them in a more favorable light.

Lists of Endangered Species

Different countries, as well as international conservation organizations, maintain lists of endangered plant and animal species. In the United States, the Endangered Species Act of 1973 is administered by the Fish and Wildlife Service. The service considers up-to-date information about the population status of a species when it decides whether to list that species as endangered or threatened.

The Convention on International Trade in Endangered Species of Wild Fauna and Flora (CITES) is a multinational agreement that regulates trade in certain plant and animal species in order to prevent their overexploitation. As of 2000, CITES maintained a list that contained over twenty-five hundred animal species and over thirty thousand plant species. The CITES list contains three categories: species that are threatened with extinction that are or may be affected by trade; species that are not threatened but may become so unless trade is controlled; and species that any of the 118 member nations wish to protect within their jurisdiction and for which they need the cooperation of others in controlling trade.

bats are still critically endangered. As people try to save them, they look for ways to balance the needs and wants of growing human populations with the desire to preserve bats and their habitats.

1

Helpful Flying Mammals

FOR CENTURIES MYTHS and superstitions have surrounded bats, and they have suffered from what some people consider bad public relations. Bats were portrayed as dirty, dangerous, blood-sucking creatures that attacked humans and animals. Long ago, Europeans who saw flocks of bats rising out of underground caves at night feared them as fiends flying up from hell. When English explorer Captain James Cook and his crew arrived in Australia in 1770, one seaman described the flying fox as "a black devil with wings and horns."[1] Bats have long been associated with witches, vampires, haunted houses, and Halloween. More recently, they have been staples in gothic horror films.

Clearing up misconceptions

Scientists and bat lovers have tried to dispel the numerous misconceptions based on fear and ignorance. They point out that bats normally do not attack people and that they even avoid humans. A bat trapped inside a house may fly in a wild manner but will leave if people open windows or doors. Bats are also clean animals that groom themselves each day. Like other mammals, bats can catch rabies, but, according to the U.S. Fish and Wildlife Service, this contagious viral disease affects less than one-half of 1 percent of all bats. Rabid bats usually die quickly, and they are seldom aggressive, factors that minimize the likelihood that a rabid bat will attack people or their pets.

Do bats suck blood? A very small number of them do. There are three species of vampire bats, all native to Latin America. They are the only mammals that survive on blood alone. Their natural prey are birds and small mammals, but they have turned to easier targets—cows, horses, pigs, and goats—as people have built more farms and ranches around their habitats. These bats bite an animal and then lick the blood that flows from the wound, which is about two or

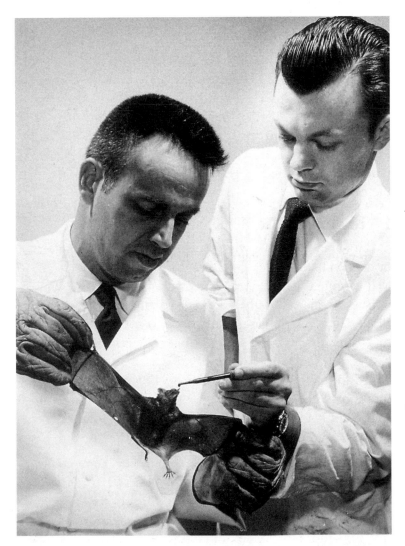

A scientist from the Cornell Zoological Research Project holds a vampire bat as his colleague provides its daily blood ration. Laypersons should not handle bats under any circumstances.

three tablespoons. Vampire bats are known for their agility. They can walk, hop, and run on their hind legs before taking off in the air.

However, the vast majority of bats are gentle creatures who are quite helpful to humankind. They eat pests that harm crops and forests and that spread diseases among humans. Bats also pollinate plants and trees and aid medical research.

Scientists believe that bats have lived on the earth since Eocene times, over 50 million years ago, and that they have not changed much physically since then. They are unsure about the bat's ancestors and evolutionary history. They have not located fossils of creatures that resemble both bats and other animals. Bats themselves do not fossilize well because of their small size and light bones. In any case, they have concluded that bats did not evolve from rodents, the order that includes mice and rats. They may have evolved from a small, nocturnal, shrewlike mammal that lived in forests and fed on insects. Bats have unique features, and their bodies are well suited to the way they live.

Flying mammals

Bats are mammals, which means they have teeth and fur or hair on their bodies. Like other mammals, bats give birth to live young, which a mother bat nurses with her milk.

Bats are also the only mammals capable of true, sustained flight. Certain familiar animals, such as some kinds of squirrels, glide through the air and thus appear to be flying, but bats can actually fly, like birds do, as the actions of their wings lift them into the air and propel them forward. Unlike birds, bats do not fly over the open ocean, and nearly all species of bats fly at night, not during the day. Bats can maneuver their bodies while flying, which helps them to catch insects or find other kinds of food.

Some bat species rely on flight mostly to get from place to place, while others use it mostly for hunting and feeding. The ability to fly is also critically important for helping bats escape from certain predators.

Bats' wingspans range from about six inches for the unusually tiny bumblebee bat to six and a half feet for the golden-crowned fruit bat. A bat's wings may look frail because they are often translucent, but they actually have strong muscles and tough membranes. The bones that give shape to these wings are actually four long, stretched-out finger bones. For this reason, scientists have given bats their own order: Chiroptera, which means "hand-wing" or "hand-winged."

Although a bat's wings look fragile, they contain strong muscles. Most bats have a claw on each wing that is used for crawling, gripping, and as a cutting tool.

Bats, Large and Small

Along with their wide variety of physical features, bats come in different sizes. They range in body length from one inch to sixteen inches.

The largest bats are flying foxes, which eat fruit and often live on islands. These bats can weigh two to three pounds, and their wings may measure more than six feet from end to end. The samoan flying fox, giant flying fox, and golden crown flying fox are also among the world's largest bats. The latter two species live in the Philippines.

The smallest bat, called the hog-nosed bat or the bumblebee bat, is about the same size as a bumblebee and weighs about as much as one grape, with a wingspan of about six inches. This tiny, insectivorous bat, which can fit on two fingers of a human hand, is the smallest mammal on the earth, next to the shrew. These bats live in Thailand, where people once collected them as souvenirs. The International Union for the Conservation of Nature and Natural Resources has placed this bat on its list of the twelve most endangered animals in the world.

Other small bats include the tiny Philippine bamboo bat, which weighs only one-twentieth of an ounce and measures about one and a half inches in length. The pipestrelle (from the Italian word *pipistrello*, which means "bat") weighs about one-fifth of an ounce. These bats are found in both North and South America, Africa, and Europe, and they tend to roost in cliffs and rocky areas, usually alone. They eat insects, including beetles, moths, mosquitoes, and leafhoppers.

A tiny bumblebee bat is shown nestled in a scientist's hand. Only those specifically trained to do so should handle bats.

Most bats also have a single claw on the front of each wing that aids in walking or crawling and serves as a cutting tool. The unique system of tendons in the bat's toes enables it to grip things firmly with its claws. These clawed toes also help bats to sleep upside down with their feet wrapped around a roost. Some bats cling to a roost with just one claw.

A slow rate of reproduction

Most species of bats, particularly those living in temperate regions, mate during the fall or early winter, but the male bat's sperm remains dormant in the female's body. Fertilization does not take place until early spring, after the female bat has emerged from hibernation. Females then move to roosting sites, where they form maternity colonies. Their pups are born in late spring or summer.

Most bat species produce only one offspring each year, a low rate of reproduction compared to most animals. A few species of bats have more than one pup in a litter. For instance, the big brown bats of eastern North America often bear twins, and red bats, which also live in North America, may have three or even four offspring at a time. In addition to this low birth rate, fewer than 50 percent of all bat pups survive to adulthood. Also, some females do not give birth until they are two or more years old. These factors make bats especially vulnerable to declining numbers.

Mother bats nurse their pups longer than other mammals, usually until they are nearly full grown. This helps young bats to survive until their wings are large and strong and they are able to obtain food on their own. Some species are full grown and can fly by the time they reach the age of three to five weeks. Bats live anywhere from five to twenty or thirty years.

Useful facial features

Although the bodies of bats are basically very similar, different species have diverse facial features—such as skull shapes, noses, mouths, jaws, teeth, and ears—that make their heads look quite different. These features are both unusual and useful.

Bats' noses come in diverse shapes and sizes and sometimes have special sensing abilities. For example, the tube-nosed bat has a small circular structure that looks like a short section of a soda straw on the tip of its nose. Other bats have nasal structures that resemble leaves, horns, swords, or flowers. Bats' snouts may be short or long, depending on what they eat. Bats that forage for pollen deep inside a blossom have long, slender snouts.

Bats' teeth also vary, depending on their diets. For instance, bats that eat small animals have prominent canine teeth and two or three molars. Insect eaters have W-shaped cheek teeth that enable them to slice and crush their prey. In some species, such as free-tailed bats, the lower incisors are used like a comb for grooming the fur.

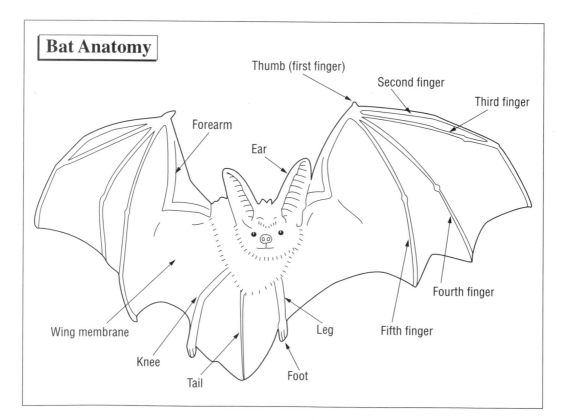

Bat Anatomy

Thumb (first finger)

Second finger

Third finger

Forearm

Ear

Fourth finger

Fifth finger

Wing membrane

Leg

Knee

Tail

Foot

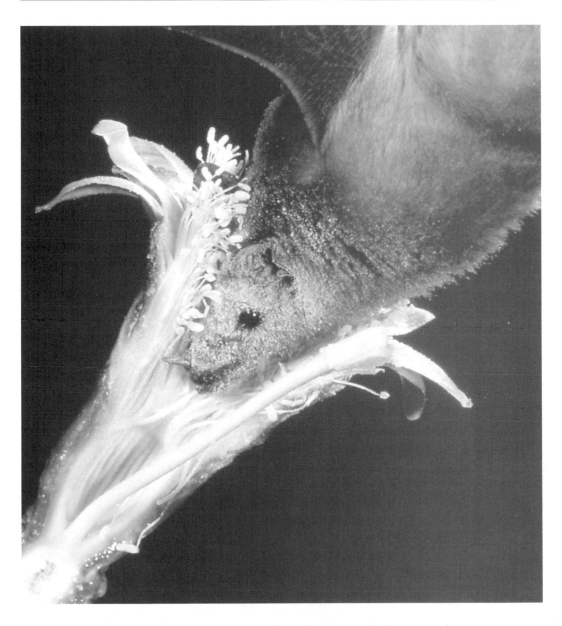

Most bats' ears are large compared to the rest of the head, and they, too, come in an array of shapes and sizes. One of the most interesting sets of ears belongs to the spotted bat, a rarely seen species that lives in desert scrub and open forest areas in western North America, including Yosemite National Park. Behind two fleshy appendages, the spotted bat has ears that looks like large butterfly

This lesser long-nosed bat has a long, slim snout, which allows it to plunge its nose into a blossom's center to feast on pollen.

The spotted bat's large ears, located behind fleshy appendages, aid in navigation at night.

wings. These ears are a pale pinkish gray color, and they help the spotted bat navigate in the dark.

Ear size is thought to be an indication off how much a bat relies on its hearing or its other senses to get around. Fruit bats tend to have smaller ears, and scientists think this is because a sense of smell plays the primary role for creatures hunting for fruits and plants, which have distinctive odors but do not move.

Bat radar

Bats' ears help them find their way around by using a sort of bat radar. Italian scientist Lazarro Spallanzani suggested this idea around 1790, after he noticed that pipestrelle bats could avoid obstacles in a dark room without using their senses of vision, smell, or touch.

Bats use echolocation, a natural form of sonar similar to that used by dolphins and whales. They fly with their mouths open and send out a series of high-pitched, loud, squeaking sounds that bounce off the objects around them. Most of these noises are at frequencies too high for humans to hear. According to bat researcher Alvin Novick, "I measured the pulses of a Malayan naked free-tailed bat—an animal about as big as a bluejay—at 145 decibels. That's comparable to the sound level of some jets at takeoff."[2]

Insect-eating bats use echolocation to home in on insects in flight or to find them on the surfaces of leaves and trees. Fishing bats use echolocation as a guide to ripples on the water that indicate the presence of fish.

The ability to detect and locate sounds also enables bats to avoid bumping into things. Merlin D. Tuttle, a zoologist and the founder of Bat Conservation International, says, "Bats can perceive motion, distance, speed, trajectory, and shape. They can detect and avoid obstacles no thicker than a human hair."[3]

Bats that rely on echolocation have larger ears and smaller eyes. However, bats are not blind—another legend that has surrounded these creatures. In fact, many bats have good vision, and those bats usually have fairly large eyes.

Feeding habits

In general, bats have large appetites because their flying bodies use a great deal of energy. Some bats eat several times their weight in food each night, and nursing females must consume even more because they require extra energy to produce milk. For example, a lactating Mexican free-tailed bat eats about 1.2 times her body weight in food each day, and her baby consumes its own weight in milk. Certain bat species eat several different things while others have more restricted diets. A broad diet may help particular species to survive.

Insectivorous bats—those that eat insects—are found in every part of the world where bats live. Most bats, including nearly all of the species found in the United States and

A Devoted Advocate

Perhaps the best-known bat scientist and conservationist in the United States is Merlin D. Tuttle. A mammalogist by training, he has studied bats since the 1960s and founded Bat Conservation International in 1982. Tuttle has done a great deal to educate people around the world about bats and to promote conservation programs.

Tuttle's interest in animals dates back to childhood, when he reared monarch butterflies and took part in the nature classes his biologist father taught at Yosemite National Park. When the family moved to Tennessee during Tuttle's junior year in high school, he began studying bats at a nearby cave. During college he visited hundreds of bat caves around North America.

In addition to his publications and frequent speeches, Tuttle, also known as "the Bat Man," is a famous bat photographer. He has captured the images of hundreds of bats from around the world by using creative methods that do not frighten the bats and often show them in their habitats.

In an article titled "Photographing the World's Bats," which appeared in a 1988 issue of *Bats Magazine*, Tuttle explained,

> Because of their shy nature and nocturnal habits, bats are exceptionally difficult to portray photographically as they really are in the wild. When first captured, they either try to fly away, bare their teeth in a threat display, or hunker down, eyes closed, expecting the worst. Impatient photographers typically held a bat by its wings, blew in its face and snapped a quick picture when the bat tried to defend itself with a snarl.

Tuttle's photographs have helped to change the image of bats.

Dr. Merlin D. Tuttle removes a nectar-eating bat from a net in a cave.

about 70 percent worldwide, eat insects. These bats usually capture their prey in flight and use their wings or a flap of skin between the hind legs to catch them. They may focus on one or more kinds of insects.

Other bats eat fruits, pollen, or nectar. Fruit-eating bats, which live in the tropics, have strong, long teeth to cut through rinds and dig into the fruit. The brains of fruit bats

A lesser long-nosed bat feeds on cardon fruit. The brains of fruit bats are relatively large, enabling them to remember where and when fruit can be found.

are relatively large. Scientists think this gives them the capacity to remember both where to find fruits and when those fruits will be ripe. Bats that feed on nectar and pollen are uncommon, especially in the Old World. They can be found in California, Arizona, and Texas.

A small number of species eat fish or small animals. In Latin America false vampire bats, which are the largest bats in the Western Hemisphere, eat rodents, birds, lizards, and smaller species of bats; meanwhile, fringe-lipped bats attack frogs along with other prey. Blood-feeding bats are found only in Central and South America. The bulldog bat of Central America feeds on fish during the dry season but eats insects during the rainy months of the year.

Bat diets help people and plants

The insect-eating bats are more important in pest control than any other group of mammals or birds. Mosquitoes are a favorite prey. A single bat can eat thousands of mosquitoes in one night, and just one small brown bat may eat as many as six hundred per hour. According to Tuttle, "The 20 million free-tailed bats from Bracken Cave in Central Texas, eat a quarter of a million pounds or more of insects in a single night!"[4]

Besides mosquitoes, bat species eat moths, beetles, flies, stink bugs, leafhoppers, root worms, and other pests, many of which can damage crops. A colony of bats can eat about 15 million root worms in a summer, thus providing farmers with a reliable and nontoxic form of pest control.

Bats that eat fruits and nectar play a key role in propagating such useful crop plants as mangoes, bananas, avocados, dates, guavas, peaches, breadfruit, figs, carob, cloves, and cashews. As bats dip into the flowers to sip nectar, their wings brush against the stamens of many flowers and pick up pollen. The bats then distribute this pollen to the next plant they visit, thus ensuring another season's growth to a plant that might otherwise have gone unfertilized.

In fact, bats are the only animals that can pollinate certain plants, such as the balsa. The lightweight wood from this tree, which grows from Mexico to southern Bolivia, is

Frog-Eating Bats

A type of frog-eating species called the fringe-lipped bat lives on Barro Colorado Island in Panama. This bat finds male mud-puddle frogs at ponds by listening to the frogs' mating calls. Even a faint noise from the frog will enable a bat to locate it, swoop down, and capture it with its mouth.

During the early 1980s bat expert Merlin D. Tuttle studied these bats in their habitats. He was excited by some of the findings he made by playing tape-recorded frog calls to the bats. By listening to the frog calls, the bats were able to determine what kinds of frogs made various sounds. They were drawn toward the calls made by frogs that were small enough to eat as well as to the calls of nonpoisonous (and therefore edible) species of frogs. In an article for *National Geographic* titled "The Amazing Frog-Eating Bat," Tuttle writes, "We determined that our bats could also distinguish between the calls of frogs of edible size and those that are too large to eat."

Other frog-eating species—Indian false vampire bats, heart-nosed bats, and large slit-faced bats—locate their prey by listening to the frogs' movements, not their calls. They attack frogs on land rather than on the water.

A frog-eating bat zeros in on its prey, a red-eyed tree frog.

Lesser long-nosed bats pollinate a saguaro cactus flower.

used to make canoes and model airplanes. In the southwestern United States, bats pollinate organ-pipe and saguaro cacti. The body shape of one bat species enables the animal to make contact with both the pollen-bearing parts of the flower of the balsa tree and the pollen-receiving parts in order to propagate the tree. Bats are also the only animals that pollinate the ceiba, or silk cotton tree. This tree, found in the American tropics, provides useful wood, oil, and seeds. While sucking out the nectar of one ceiba tree, bats deposit the pollen of trees visited earlier. In the savannahs of eastern Africa, bats alone can pollinate the baobab tree, whose flowers open at night. The bats approach the flower from below to obtain nectar, and, in the process, they make contact with the reproductive organs of that plant. The baobab is called "the Tree of Life" because it supports many other forms of wildlife in the region.

Bats' roles in ecology

In addition to directly aiding plant reproduction by means of pollination, bats help to regenerate forests by spreading seeds. For instance, a species of flying foxes that live in West Africa spread the seeds of the iroko tree, the source of millions of dollars in timber each year.

After gathering fruits, bats often carry fruits elsewhere before they eat them in order to escape from predators. The seeds from these fruits are excreted from the bats as they fly through the air. Seeds fall on new ground, often in an open space where they will have enough sunlight to grow. Furthermore, bats spread the seeds of wild plants. Wild plants often resist disease and insects better than cultivated plants. In some cases, bats are the only animals that disperse the seeds of a particular plant.

Edward Stashko, a biologist who has studied bats, says, "Bats are one of the main animals responsible for maintaining tropical rain forests. People are not very aware of the role of bats."[5] Scientists estimate that bats account for 95 percent of the reforestation process in tropical rain forests. The rain forests are important in the ecology of the

When a lush tropical rain forest such as this one is destroyed by man or nature, bats play a highly significant role in reforestation.

earth, so bat activity in these regions affects people and animals everywhere.

Even bat droppings, called guano, help humankind. In its natural state, guano can serve as a rich fertilizer. Some people, especially in developing countries, collect guano for their farms and gardens. Monks living at a monastery in Southeast Asia harvest guano and sell it to local farmers, earning about one hundred thousand dollars each year from this endeavor. Likewise, bat guano is processed and used in products that detoxify industrial wastes and also to make the fuel gasohol.

Bats and medical research

Bats have also contributed to improved health care for both humans and animals. Scientists have discovered bacteria in guano that may prevent diseases in animals. They are extracting certain bacteria from guano and using these organisms to make antibiotics that can fight infectious diseases.

Furthermore, scientists have been investigating the anticoagulant substance found in the saliva of vampire bats. This substance prevents the blood of their victims from clotting quickly. The substance has been shown to open clogged arteries faster than the medicines that are currently on the market. Researchers think it might be used in a medication for people with heart disease and may even help to prevent heart attacks.

Bat expert Tuttle sums up several ways in which bat research has aided the health care field:

> Studies of bats have contributed to the development of navigational aids for the blind, birth control and artificial insemination techniques, vaccine production, and drug testing, as well as to a better understanding of low-temperature surgical procedures.[6]

Scientists stress the importance of protecting bats and their roosting places so that further research can take place.

Roosts and colonies

For bats, survival centers around roosts. Bats need both summer roosts, with climate conditions suitable for raising their young, and winter sites, where they can hibernate undisturbed without freezing to death. In addition, sources of food and water must be within flying distance of the roosts.

Bats make their home in an old ivy-covered tower in Surrey, England.

Bats live in many different places. They find roosting places in nature or in places made by humans for other purposes. These include barns, churches, and other buildings (attics or roofs), bridges, and mines. In some places, bats live in ancient tombs, abandoned monasteries, and military bunkers; elsewhere, they cluster around monuments. Some bats live in houses that humans build just for them. Bat houses can be found in public parks, wooded areas, and on private property.

Most bats are social animals that roost in groups throughout the year or for part of the year. Colonies may consist of anywhere from a few bats to tens of thousands of bats to even a million or more. Bats usually remain with the colonies into which they were born. Some types of bats also form families, and the male and female may stay together throughout their lives. Still other kinds of bats, such as the northern yellow bat, are solitary.

Scientists have observed many instances of bats helping each other. For example, some female bats share their food with others in their roost when the nursing females are not well enough to hunt for food on their own. Bats may also look out for each other's pups and vampire bats sometimes adopt motherless pups.

Caves and trees provide the majority of natural roosts. Bats live in different parts of trees, including the branches, leaves, or bark. Others find homes in woodpecker holes or hollow trunks. Bats also nest in rock crevices, animal burrows, tall jungle grasses, clumps of moss, or even spider webs. Solitary bats choose homes under bark and rock crevices or among leaves.

Millions of bats live in caves, including three species of endangered bats in the United States: gray bats, Indiana bats, and Ozark big-eared bats. These species winter inside caves while hanging in large clusters. When spring arrives, female gray bats form small maternity colonies, often under loose tree bark. Indiana bats and Ozark big-eared bats move to different caves.

Migration and hibernation

Bats living in cold climates—for example, the northern United States and Canada—may migrate south during the winter. As winter approaches, bats that do not fly south prepare to hibernate. The foods they consume are not available during the cold winter months, and they must conserve their energy.

Hibernating bats leave the trees or bat houses they used during the summer and relocate to mines, caves, or other, more unexpected, places. The red bats of North America have been found hibernating in piles of leaf litter that fell during autumn.

By the time they begin hibernating, bats have stored up about 35 percent of their body weight in fat. They live off the fat stored in their bodies and do not require nearly as much oxygen as active bats. Some bats hibernate as long as six or seven months.

Hibernation is a critical period in the life cycle of many bat species. The major threat facing the Indiana bat is its vulnerability during the hibernation period. These bats can only survive the winter if temperatures remain within the extremely narrow range of thirty-nine to forty-three degrees Fahrenheit (twenty-one to twenty-five degrees Celsius). When the temperatures rise higher, the bats wake up when their prey are unavailable and end up using too much of their body fat reserves; colder temperatures cause them to freeze. Such strict requirements make it hard for Indiana bats to find just the right places to hibernate.

If all goes well during the hibernation period, bats can survive the winter. However, disaster may strike, in the form of attacks from predators or mine cave-ins, as well as other forms of habitat destruction.

2

Enemies

PREDATION—BY BOTH natural predators and humans—
has reduced the number of bats, eliminating some species
altogether, endangering others, and threatening still others
with extinction. Hunting and other human activities, such
as the use of pesticides, endanger bats. Humans also disrupt
bats or their habitats and roosts in ways that drive them
away or cause them to die.

Threats from disease and natural disasters

Fear of disease is a factor that contributes to the once
prevalent image of bats as dangerous, and bats can indeed
transmit certain viruses. In 1998 a woman in Australia who
was caring for a sick bat died from infection of Australian
bat lyssavirus (ABL). This disease, which is related to rabies, occurs all over the world and affects different kinds
of mammals. To avoid catching such diseases, bat han-
dlers are urged to wear gloves if they must handle a bat
and to have a rabies vaccination, which also protects
against ABL.

For the most part, however, viruses like ABL and rabies
are more harmful to bats than to people. As bat expert Merlin D. Tuttle says,

> They are rarely rabid, and even then are seldom aggressive.
> When people are bitten, it is usually because they have picked
> up a sick individual that bites in self-defense. Bats found
> where they can be picked up should be assumed to be sick
> and left alone.[7]

Bats can die as a result of accidents and natural disasters, including severe storms or temperatures that are too high or too low inside the caves and mines where they are hibernating. Cave flooding can also drown large numbers of hibernating bats. For example, about three hundred thousand Indiana bats drowned in cave floodings during the early 1960s. Caves may also collapse, killing the bats inside or blocking the entrances.

In addition, certain regions are regularly pummeled by major storms. For instance, severe typhoons strike the Pacific islands of Samoa about every three years, and this has contributed to the decline of endangered species of fruit bats. Likewise, forest fires kill bats and other animals, both directly and by destroying their habitats. But these are not the only sources of danger to the world's bat populations.

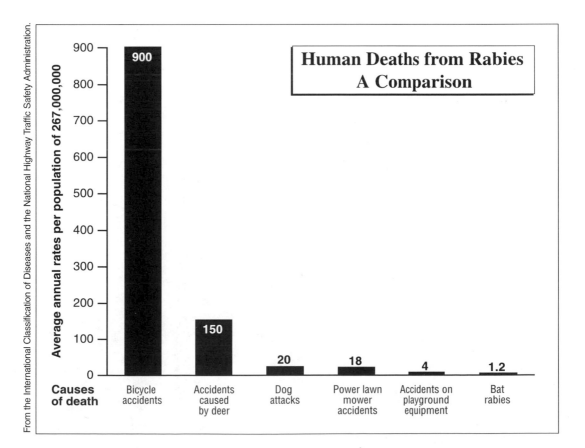

From the International Classification of Diseases and the National Highway Traffic Safety Administration.

The Endangered Indiana Bat

The small- to medium-size Indiana bat lives primarily in caves located in Kentucky, Indiana, Missouri, Arkansas, and parts of New England. Most of the remaining population inhabits eight caves and one mine scattered around these states. The fur of this species is a dull gray or brownish color with a pinkish underside. Indiana bats feed on mosquitoes and agricultural pests, such as cucumber beetles, leafhoppers, and june bugs. They also help to protect forests by eating tent caterpillar moths.

Indiana bats were placed on the U.S. Fish and Wildlife Service's endangered species list in 1967, and their numbers have further declined by about 34 percent since 1983. Between 1991 and 2000, the number of these bats is thought to have decreased from about five hundred thousand to three hundred thousand. In an ABC News segment called "Ancient Bat Clues," Rick Toomey, a paleontologist at the Illinois State Museum, said, "If we don't do something soon, we will lose them in our lifetime."

The bats' primary enemy is humans. People exploring caves have disturbed hibernating Indiana bats. Scientists say that insecticide poisoning and the use of bats as laboratory animals have further contributed to their decline.

To protect these bats, the National Park Service has fenced in hibernation caves in the Ozark National Forest and Buffalo National River lands. The public was banned from entering these areas and signs were posted to inform people about protecting bat colonies.

The Indiana bat is highly endangered, due largely to human interference with its habitat.

Threats from natural predators

Bats have enemies in the wild. Their natural predators include skunks, raccoons, snakes, opossums, foxes, weasels, bobcats, civets, and mongooses, which kill bats for food, usually by catching them while they are roosting. Falcons, owls, hawks, crows, blackbirds, and blue jays are among the birds that prey on bats. Even house cats and dogs have been observed attacking and killing bats. Young bats that fall from their roosts to the ground sometimes become food for ants and roaches.

Studies of Mammoth Cave in Kentucky show that raccoons and other predators once had a fairly easy time capturing Indiana bats, an endangered species that once numbered in the millions. These bats hibernate in dense groups of about 350 bats or more per square foot. During the 1800s so many bats lived in the cave that raccoons and other predators could reach the bats and eat them at will.

This unfortunate Rhoad's bat makes a tasty meal for a snake.

The extinction of the Lord Howe Island bat in Australia has been blamed on predators introduced into the region by people who did not anticipate the effect of this action on the local bats. During the early 1900s Norwegian rats from a shipwrecked vessel swam to Lord Howe Island, where they began to attack bats. To control the rats, people brought owls to Australia, but these birds also preyed on the bats. Since the bats had evolved in such a small, isolated place, unchallenged by either rats or owls, they had no natural defenses against the new predators. Helpless against these two new threats, the bats became extinct.

Other Australian bats have been killed by the European fox, feral cats, and cane toads, all of which were brought to Australia from Europe. Feral cats and cane toads attack bats as they fly out of underground roosts.

Predators also kill bats in New Zealand, another island country in the southwestern Pacific Ocean. The greater short-tailed bat may be extinct, and the lesser short-tailed bat is endangered. Both types live mainly in lowland forests and are among the most terrestrial bats. Although these bats do catch some of their food in flight, they find most of their food on tree trunks or on the forest floor. They use their rear legs and feet, as well as their forearms, to walk. This makes them more vulnerable to predators like the Polynesian rat, which arrived with the Maori who settled on these islands about one thousand years ago.

Besides Polynesian rats, these bats are also killed by ship rats, Norwegian rats, ferrets, feral cats, and weasels. Weasels were brought to New Zealand to kill rabbits. Ship rats and weasel-like animals called stoats are thought to have destroyed the most bats and large numbers of ground-nesting birds.

Threats related to natural predators

Now New Zealand's bats face a threat involving a growing population of possums. Brought to the island during the 1800s to build a fur industry, the Australian brushtail opossum has also thrived outside the fur-breeding farms. Many thousands of opossums live in various forests and

The Greater Mouse-Eared Bat

The greater mouse-eared bat is threatened and seems to be extinct now in Britain. These bats were plentiful in Europe, especially the Netherlands, Belgium, and Poland, until about 1950. By the 1990s few of these animals could be found in north-western Europe.

Greater mouse-eared bats, which eat moths and beetles, are relatively large and live about six or seven years. They tend to be solitary, although males may live in small groups during the summer, and female bats form large nursery colonies, either in caves or buildings.

The bats have declined as a result of disturbances in their caves, which range from human vandalism, to unregulated tourism and exploration, to waste disposal. Agricultural chemicals, especially insecticides, have also played a part in their decline.

Most European countries have passed laws designed to protect these bats and their habitats. In Germany and the Netherlands, people have also worked hard to create new roosting places for them.

often roam onto farmlands, where people try to catch them with jawed traps or kill them with cyanide poison, using fruit essences to attract animals. Animal activists fear that bats could be lured by the bait or could blunder into the traps, but the impact of these measures is unclear.

Bats also sicken and die from parasite infestation. Ticks pose the most danger, and these parasites usually attach to bats that fly close to the ground. Researchers have found that ticks usually attack bats at their feeding sites rather than at their roosts.

During the late 1980s Australians living on the Atherton Tablelands, a part of Queensland, noticed that spectacled flying foxes were dying for some unexplained reason. Further investigation showed that these bats were dying as a result of tick bites received between October and December each year. These flying foxes, which are large in size,

The spectacled flying fox is one bat species vulnerable to fatal tick bites.

fly low to feed on the flowers of the tobacco plant. Ticks that spend time on these plants hop onto the bats and bite them, releasing a toxin that paralyzes the bats, robbing them of their ability to fly. Trapped on the ground and unable to escape predators or seek food and water, they die.

The number of spectacled flying foxes has declined greatly in recent years. This species, which has the most restricted distribution of any flying fox in Australia, plays a key role in the regeneration of the rain forest in north

Queensland. These fast-flying bats are the only mammals that can rapidly disperse seeds from one rain forest tract to another. Unfortunately, the spectacled flying fox is also under threat due to loss of habitat, shooting and poisoning by orchard owners and other people, and birth abnormalities.

Human hunters

Because most bats are so small, humans do not typically hunt them for their fur or skin. Likewise, their teeth and other body parts do not yield enough ivory or other materials to make them valuable prey. However, in some ancient societies, such as the Inca and Aztec cultures, high-ranking people did decorate their clothing with bat fur, which was harvested by slave labor.

In modern times, humans harm bats both on purpose and unintentionally. In Africa, Asia, and on islands in the Pacific and Indian Oceans, people hunt bats for food. Usually, they hunt larger species of fruit bats, such as the megabat,

A restaurateur spreads the wings of a bat on the menu at a wild animal restaurant in Ho Chi Minh City, Vietnam.

which is found on Guam. In some parts of Africa, people hunt and eat the straw-colored fruit bat, which is considered a delicacy, and they hunt other large species of fruit bats for food.

Hunters do not usually kill enough bats to endanger the survival of a species. However, hunting can have a big impact when a particular species lives only in a limited region. Also, when nursing mothers are killed, their pups then die from starvation.

On Guam, Mariana fruit bats, which are called *fanihi*, have traditionally been eaten as a delicacy on important occasions, such as weddings and feasts. Years ago, natives caught these bats using either long poles with nooses attached to the ends or with traps. However, when people began killing the bats with firearms, the population began to decline more rapidly than the bats could reproduce. In fact, so many bats were killed, or died for other reasons, that people on Guam began importing them from other Pacific islands. The survival of these bats is now threatened because poachers have disobeyed laws that ban people from killing or harassing them.

In some cases, humans conducting research have killed the very bats they wanted to study—for example, to learn more about them or to improve conservation methods. Scientists trying to identify poorly known species usually examine their teeth and skulls carefully. They may even analyze the bats' cells and tissues. These research techniques, of course, cannot be performed on living animals. According to author M. Brock Fenton, "Many studies on the distribution and classification of bats require specimens [that is, dead bats], which usually are added to museum collections." Fenton also points out, "Some studies of bat echolocation use procedures that are fatal to bats. This is particularly true of research into information processing in bats' brains."[8]

Killing bats labeled as pests

Farmers also sometimes kill fruit bats, usually flying foxes, that come into their orchards to feed. In Australia,

Bat Trappers in the Philippines

Human activities, such as hunting and destroying forests, threaten bats in the Philippines, a group of about seven thousand islands in the Pacific Ocean. The Philippine tube-nosed bat is critically endangered. It is expected to become extinct by 2015 unless the remaining population is protected. The Panay fruit bat is also endangered.

People on some Philippine islands, where sources of food are limited, hunt and eat certain species of fruit bats, which may be one of their few available sources of protein. In some places, bats are sold in grocery stores as a delicacy. People on certain islands also believe that these bats have special powers and that men will be stronger and more virile if they eat them.

New laws were passed in 1995 to halt large-scale hunting, but trappers still catch and kill numerous bats. They block cave entrances for several days, then capture the bats in nets when they come out for food and water.

Conservation groups consider the Philippines to be a high priority, and they are working to educate people about the vital role bats play in pollinating many kinds of plants. Scientists have presented lectures on bat conservation at schools, and conservation groups have distributed posters that inform people about bats.

for example, bats fly into commercial orchards to suck nectar and eat mangoes, litchi nuts, papayas, peaches, nectarines, and other fruits. These bats once depended on wild flowering trees and ripe rain forest fruits, but as these trees disappeared, they adapted and began commuting to the suburbs and cities at night to find food. Author Derek Grzelewski describes the current situation:

> Trouble comes when this movable feast fails due to drought, flood, or fire. In the past, the four Australian species of flying fox could move on to other forests. With large-scale land clearing for agriculture and housing, the bats have nowhere to go. Swarms of desperately hungry bats descend on urban gardens and fruit trees, where they become pests.[9]

In attempts to prevent further destruction of their crops, Australian farmers have eliminated large numbers of bats by shooting them and poisoning them with strychnine.

They have killed others with networks of electrified wires above the orchards, which electrocute the bats, and

Fire is one threat to bat habitat and food supply.

by burning them with flamethrowers. They even considered introducing the typhoid virus into bat colonies in order to get rid of them. Farmers have also tried using loud noises and high-powered lights to deter bats, but after a day or two, the bats returned in spite of the noises and lights.

Orchard owners in the Philippines have also used different methods to kill fruit bats. They destroyed so many bare-backed fruit bats that this species, and certain other fruit bat species, became extinct.

Humans sometimes kill bats they find living in their attics or barns, frequently with poison. Chlorophacinone (Rozol) is often used for this purpose. Scientists have warned people that exposure to this substance may also be harmful to humans.

Killing bats that are not pests

In Central and South America, people kill bats out of fear, ignorance, and prejudice. They regard vampire bats as threats to people, livestock, and crops and fear them as carriers of rabies and other diseases. They have also blasted thousands of caves to destroy colonies of vampire bats. In Brazil more than eight thousand cave colonies were destroyed during one campaign to kill vampire bats. Mass killings aimed at vampires have also destroyed fruit bats, insectivorous bats, and other animals that happened to be occupying the same roosting places. Also, people shooting at bats in caves have accidentally killed long-nosed bats that pollinate plants.

Bats that roost in caves and abandoned mines are especially vulnerable to attack. They form large groups as they roost together and are easy to find in these enclosed spaces. Indiana bats, for instance, form large, tight clusters on cave ceilings when they hibernate. According to the Arkansas Game and Fish Commission, as many as 480 Indiana bats have been found in a space of one square foot.

A colony in Wolf River Cave in Tennessee was deliberately killed. During the winter of 1999 a caver from the area found forty Indiana and gray bats lying dead inside. It

Mexican free-tailed bats emerge from their cave. A prime roosting spot for many bats, caves are under threat from humans.

was determined that someone had thrown mud at the bats while they were hibernating in the cave. Both species are on the federal endangered species list.

Humans have destroyed far larger numbers of bats, however. A huge colony of Mexican free-tailed bats was killed in Eagle Creek Cave in Arizona. In 1963 this cave held the largest known colony of this species, about 30 million, and scientists estimated that they consumed about 350,000 pounds of insects each night. However, by 1969 only 300,000 bats remained. Shotgun casings found at the cave entrance indicated that shooters had attacked the bats. In 1976 a colony of about 250,000 gray bats living in Hambrick Cave in Alabama were slaughtered by people wielding sticks, stones, and firearms.

Human predation and disturbance have also been blamed for the endangered status of the Ozark big-eared bat, which lives in caves. People have attacked hibernating bats and nursery colonies. Only seventeen hundred of these bats were alive as of 2000. About fourteen hundred lived in eastern Oklahoma, and the rest lived in Arkansas. This bat once lived in Missouri but now appears to be extinct there.

Discussing a colony of Mexican free-tailed bats that lives in a cave in Bracken, Texas, Merlin Tuttle says, "Imagine, they cover thousands of square miles a night and destroy a quarter million pounds of insects, yet man seems bent on destroying them."[10]

Human disturbances

Sometimes humans harm bats unintentionally. Human visitation to bat roosts can disturb bats in fatal ways. While exploring caves or observing a bat colony, humans may

People visiting caves occupied by bats may startle the creatures into abandoning their roosts.

frighten bats and cause them to leave. Yet many species do not adapt easily to new surroundings, and substantial numbers of bats in an uprooted colony will fail to survive. Furthermore, if a mother bat is frightened, she may move her pup to a different part of the cave or mine where the temperature may be too cool for the pup to survive.

Caves may also be disturbed for economic reasons. In a part of southeastern Brazil, roost disturbance occurs as people obtain limestone from caves. Caves in Brazil have not been managed or controlled, and people can visit them at will, usually disturbing the bats in the process.

A colony of about twenty thousand Sanborn's long-nosed bats died in New Mexico after Colossal Cave was opened to visitors in the 1950s. The noise and activities of so many visitors were distressing to the bats, and they fled. Also, the section of the cave that female bats once used as a maternity roost became too cold for this purpose. This species has been listed as endangered since 1987.

A change in the conditions inside caves also led to the deaths of a large colony of Indiana bats at Hundred Dome Cave, a commercial cave in Kentucky. Once one hundred thousand Indiana bats spent the winter in this cave, but by the winter of 1993 scientists could find only seventeen bats. They identified the cause: a gate that had been installed to keep out nonpaying visitors had changed the temperature and airflow in the parts of the cave where the bats hibernated and they died.

Hibernating bats are especially vulnerable to disturbances. If a bat is disturbed during this time, its body temperature will rise abruptly as the bat prepares to flee from danger. If this happens too often, the bat will lose so much of its stored fat that it will die of starvation before the winter ends. According to bat expert Tuttle, "A severe winter compounded by human disturbance could spell disaster for a hibernating bat. Only three extra arousals beyond the normal could cost the bat its life."[11]

Maternity colonies—roosting mother bats with their babies—are also quite vulnerable. When people disturb these groups, the mothers may panic and drop their young

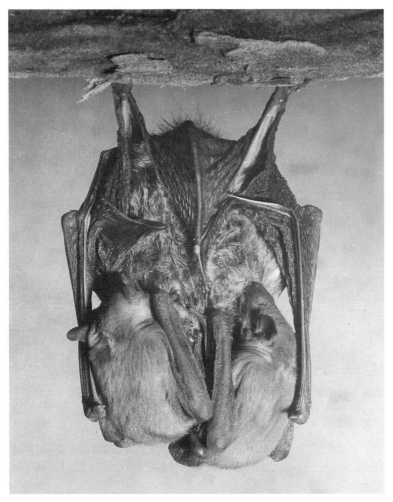

Mother bats frightened by humans may drop their young or even abandon them.

babies or abandon them. This type of disturbance contributed to the decline of the gray bat, which lives in caves in Arkansas, Missouri, Alabama, Kentucky, and Tennessee. Although there may be more than 1.5 million gray bats, nearly 95 percent of them live in just eight caves.

Researchers have found that gray bats require deep, vertical caves for hibernating during the winter. In the summer gray bats must roost in specific caves located a certain distance from rivers or reservoirs. This means that fewer than 5 percent of all available caves are suitable for their use, which puts them at greater risk than bat species that are distributed among numerous habitats.

Death and birth defects due to chemicals

Bats have also died because of the widespread use of agricultural pesticides and fertilizers, the use of certain chemicals on trees, and human-created pollution. The declining numbers of greater mouse-eared bats have been blamed, in part, on the widespread use of insecticides that can poison bats who eat plants contaminated by these chemicals.

In areas of the world where the chemical fertilizer DDT has not been banned, this poison is in some of the foods that bats eat. DDT and other pesticides that affected bats during the 1950s and 1960s are no longer used in the United States, however, and this has helped to save bats in certain regions. For example, as a result of the Clean Water Act, which banned DDT among other things, more aquatic insects are able to survive in streams. This, in turn, helps the endangered gray bats, which mainly feed on three types of aquatic insects that are highly vulnerable to pollution.

Even so, the use of any pesticides to kill insects also affects bats by reducing their food supply. Most insectivorous bats eat more than one kind of insect, however, and this flexibility can help them to survive.

Feeding on fruit contaminated with pesticides can kill bats or cause birth defects. In 1998 biologists found that spectacled flying foxes in Queensland, Australia, were being born with developmental abnormalities, such as extra digits, enlarged heads, and cleft palates. A number of the afflicted bats died shortly after birth.

Death and illness due to pollution

Human activities may harm bats by polluting their sources of drinking water. Bats have died as a result of drinking water from lakes, ponds, and streams that was contaminated with pesticides, industrial waste products, or toxic chemicals.

Bats die from other forms of environmental pollution, too. They may inhale poisonous fumes or absorb dangerous chemicals that are used around their roosts by industries and individuals.

In Australia, for instance, scientists have found high levels of lead in the tissues of flying foxes that eat fruits and live in urban areas. They think this lead comes from industrial and vehicle exhaust fumes and that bats inhale it and also ingest it when grooming their fur. Some bats have shown the effects of lead poisoning, which include weakness, inability to fly, muscle tremors, and loss of appetite. Scientists have also found high levels of fluoride in the tissues of dead insect-eating bats who live near aluminum smelters.

Bat conservationists contend that finding ways to reduce pollution and pesticide use will help humankind as a whole as well as save bats' lives.

3

Loss of Habitats and Roosts

O{\small NE OF THE} biggest threats to bats is the loss of their habitats and roosts—the places where they live and find food. Habitats include their roosting places, such as trees, buildings, rocks, chimneys, caves, mines, and bridges. It also includes the places where they forage for food, such as forests, and the swamps, ponds, streams, marshes, and drainage ditches that provide bats with sources of potable water.

Bats cannot survive or raise their young without stable roosts and safe places to hibernate during the winter. Their habitats play a key role in the way they forage for food, interact with each other, move about from season to season, and find mates. Suitable roosts also help protect bats from inclement weather and predators and enable them to conserve their energy.

Habitat loss occurs for many reasons. Sometimes bats lose their homes when old barns, churches, bridges, and other buildings or structures are demolished. Other causes of habitat loss include mine cave-ins, flooding, forest fires, and severe tropical storms as well as deforestation, real estate development, cave and mine destruction, and other human activities, such as cave exploration or building homes near old mines.

Even when forests or woodlands remain standing, changing conditions can destroy bats. Bats may leave their habitats if humans move nearby. Indeed, around the world the increasing human population is the main reason for habitat loss, for humans use the highest proportion of resources for living spaces, agriculture, and industry. And one natural resource frequently destroyed to meet human needs is forestland.

Loss of forests

Trees are among bats' most common roosting places. These include the broadleaf woodlands found in Europe, deciduous and coniferous forests found in North America, savannah woodlands found in Africa, and coastal rain forests found in Australia, the Philippines, and the Pacific islands.

Bats usually prefer primary forest, which is where the largest (and often the most valuable) trees are found. They may be quite picky about the types and locations of the

The loss of habitat, such as this California forest, remains one of the biggest threats to bats.

trees they prefer. For example, Indiana bats like to roost on species that develop loose, exfoliative bark as they age. Examples include silver maple, butternut hickory, red oak, white oak, slippery elm, and Eastern cottonwood trees.

Roosting sites on trees serve important functions for bats. During the day bats can avoid predators as they blend in with the colors and patterns of the surrounding leaves or tree trunks. Foliage may also shelter them from rain and excessive heat, depending on the size and thickness of the leaves and the size of the bat. During the night, bats that live mainly in caves or mines may roost in trees while they are eating or use a tree as a place from which to hunt. In places where winters are not too severe, bats may even hibernate in tree hollows.

Yet deforestation—the clearing of large areas of forests and woodlands—reduces habitats for bats and other animals. Deforestation has been going on for hundreds of

Peter's epauletted fruit bats roost in a thick canopy of trees. Such roosts are vital to bats as shelter from weather and as a means of hiding from predators.

Threatened: Mariana Fruit Bats

In 1998 the U.S. Fish and Wildlife Service changed the classification of the Mariana fruit bat from endangered to threatened. These fruit bats live on Guam, a U.S. territory, and in the U.S. Commonwealth of the Northern Mariana Islands. They feed on plants, mainly papaya, figs, and breadfruit.

Mariana fruit bats and little Mariana fruit bats have been the victims of illegal hunting, predation by the brown tree snake, typhoons, and the loss of habitat. Both species were listed as endangered on Guam in 1984. According to a report issued by the U.S. Fish and Wildlife Service in 2000, the last official sighting of a little Mariana fruit bat was made in 1968, so that species may be extinct.

In 1980 and 1981, author Nicholas Payne visited Rota and other islands in the region to learn more about these bats. Although laws limit the number of bats people can hunt, Payne saw that these laws were hard to enforce. In his article "Fruit Bat Off the Menu?" Payne writes,

> Unfortunately, the hunt got out of control—shooting at the roost sites did take place and more than four hunters participated. It is not known how many bats were killed but certainly large scale disturbance occurred, and only a fraction of the bats counted at the roost sites in June and August remained in October.

years, and the most extensive bat habitats were destroyed years ago.

Most deforestation occurs when people cut down trees or large areas of forest for farming, buildings, fuel, or to sell as lumber. For instance, in Australia many of the eucalyptus forests that once covered the eastern seaboard have been cleared to make way for pastures and orchards. Most of the fruit bats that once lived there are now gone.

On the island nation of Haiti, deforestation has occurred at an alarming rate, because in many parts of this impoverished Caribbean country forests offer the only source of livelihood. Bats have been casualties as people try to meet a steady demand for cleared farmland, fuel, wood, timber, and other forest products. One of these products is charcoal,

A mouse-eared bat searches for food in the forest.

which provides one of the only sources of income for people in some parts of Haiti.

The loss of forest habitats may also occur during natural disasters. For instance, in 1991 volcanic eruptions destroyed forest habitats in the Philippine Islands, and severe cyclones caused massive destruction in Bangladesh, India. Smaller areas of habitat can also be lost due to avalanches.

Brush fires have destroyed thousands of acres of forest habitat on many South Pacific islands, notably on New Caledonia and Tahiti. Some of these fires are started accidentally by farmers who are burning hillside fernland; others are set deliberately by mine operators and hunters.

The impact of deforestation on bats on islands off the African coast

The loss of forests directly affects bats. Some species of bats roost in trees while others forage in forests for their food. Some species, such as mouse-eared bats, forage only in the forest. Deforestation has put numerous bat species on the endangered species list. They include several species of fruit bats, such as the Rodrigues bat of the Mauritius Islands in the Indian Ocean.

The Livingstone's fruit bat, which lives in the Comoro Archipelago in the western Indian Ocean off the coast of Mozambique, is critically endangered because of severe deforestation. People living in this part of Africa are very poor, and they remove trees to obtain wood and land for subsistence farming. Between 1973 and 1983 about 54 percent of the primary forest in the Comoro region was lost. Although the government enacted laws against cutting down certain trees, few enforcement officers are on the job. During these same years, parts of the Comoro region were also underplanted with banana trees, and this aggravated the problems for bats.

In addition, severe cyclones ripped through the islands in 1980 and 1983, further depleting the population. Fruits were ripped from storm-damaged trees, so bats foraged for them on the ground, where they were more easily killed by

Recovering: The Rodrigues Fruit Bat

Nicknamed "the golden bat" because of the gold highlights on its brown fur, the Rodrigues fruit bat, also called the Rodrigues flying fox, was once considered quite rare. During the 1970s some scientists claimed that this species of flying fox was perhaps the rarest in the world, with no more than eighty animals left in the wild.

Rodrigues Island, which is part of Mauritius in the Indian Ocean, is located in the middle of the cyclone belt. In her 1998 article "A Personal Portrait of the Rodrigues Fruit Bat," Kim Whitman points out, "The destructive winds of this area's annual cyclones can knock bats out of trees and sweep them out to sea. Only adequate forest cover can protect the bats from Mother Nature's ire." Moreover, these bats are small and their wings are not very strong.

Although the Rodrigues fruit bat was on the verge of extinction in the 1970s, people on Rodrigues Island have worked hard to ensure the species' survival.

Since the 1980s the people on Rodrigues Island have worked to protect existing forests and have carried out reforestation programs. Habitat protection has helped these bats to survive. Laws on the island fully protect these bats, although hunters still sometimes break these laws. Rodrigues bats have also been reared in captive-breeding centers around the world.

predators. Mayotte Island has lost most of its forests as a result of both tree removal and cyclones, and fruit bats are probably extinct there.

The Pemba Island fruit bat, which lives on Pemba Island off the coast of Tanzania in the western Indian Ocean, is critically endangered. Scientists believe this bat, which may be the only species on the island that distributes larger seeds, will become extinct in the wild in the immediate future.

Pemba Island fruit bats roost in large, mature trees that are typically found in primary and secondary forests. Deforestation for agriculture and land development is the most serious threat to their survival, and hunting has also taken its toll. Because the soil in this region is so poor, people move frequently to start new farms. The human population has also been growing rapidly, raising the demand for timber for building.

The impact of deforestation on bats from Asia to Canada

Deforestation is common in Asian countries, which often have dense human populations. Although bats are often revered in Asia and are associated with good luck, some species are endangered. In Japan, logging and clearing forests to plant fruit and sugarcane have decreased habitats for fruit bats. The Ryuku flying fox is one of the endangered bats in Japan, and the Okinawa fruit bat has been declared extinct. In Taiwan, the Taiwanese fruit bat is also considered extinct. Habitat loss, along with heavy hunting during the 1980s, was the cause.

Loss of forest habitats has also contributed to the decline of two bats that live in New Zealand and eat insects, nectar, and fruit: the greater short-tailed bat, which may be extinct, and the lesser short-tailed bat, which is endangered. Bats are the only endemic land mammals in that country.

The lesser short-tailed bats have lost their habitats due to logging. These bats are known to live in three parts of that country, and about seven thousand live in the Rangataua Forest on Ruapehu. Amazingly, during the day around fifty-five hundred of the bats roost together in the hollow of one old red beech tree. The remaining members of the colony roost in three or more other trees. Scientists have learned that the females all share the same maternity roost and that the colony moves from tree to tree during the summer, following a seasonal pattern.

Brazil, too, has suffered a devastating loss of forest. For example, the Brazilian Atlantic Forest is now only about 5 percent of its original size. Three species of bats living in that forest are endangered and cannot be found anywhere else in the world.

In British Columbia, pallid bats have lost their habitats in the sagebrush steppe and ponderosa pine forest as these

A clear-cut temperate rainforest on Vancouver Island, B.C., provides an example of poor human judgment regarding the environment.

areas have been converted to make way for housing development and golf courses. Grazing by cattle has also reduced the open forage areas that these bats prefer.

Diminished food sources

Deforestation also diminishes the food supply for some bats. When food sources become scarce in the wild, bats are more likely to enter fruit orchards or other populated areas, where they risk being shot or poisoned. Likewise, those that fly close to the ground to eat fallen fruit are easier prey for animals and hunters.

In addition, fruits located on commercial orchards or farms may be sprayed with pesticides that kill the bats. Australian biologists blamed pesticides for the increase in birth defects and deaths they found among spectacled flying foxes in 1998. They said that habitat loss had forced pregnant bats to feed on fruits sprayed with chemicals. Although this species is not endangered, conservationists warn that declining numbers could pose problems because these bats play a major role in pollinating trees and dispersing seeds.

The loss of rain forest decreases the number of fruit trees for fruit bats. In the Philippines, various species of fruit bats, including Subic fruit bats, have suffered from the loss of fruit trees. These bats, which disperse the seeds of mangoes, bananas, avocados, and hundreds of other plants on the forest floor, have had to forage in places where hunters are more likely to spot them. Hunters kill them for food.

In the Pacific islands of Samoa, major typhoons have destroyed fruit trees. More than 90 percent of primary forest was defoliated during a storm that hit in December 1991. Many fruit bats starved after this storm, and others were killed when they entered plantations or villages searching for food.

Bats in the regions of Negros and Panay in the Philippines have also lost many food sources as fruit trees have been cut down. Scientists have determined that these bats must travel longer distances each night than their ancestors did on their feeding forays.

Major typhoons, such as this one viewed from space, have devastated rain forest fruit trees and greatly reduced the food supply of fruit bats.

Insectivorous bats also face declining food supplies. When pasture and grassland are converted for other uses, the number and variety of insects dwindle. The greater mouse-eared bat is among the insect-eating species whose food supplies have dwindled as foraging grounds have been converted for housing or other uses.

In addition to these other problems, bats in search of new food sources also have to fly longer and farther, which uses more energy. Working harder to obtain the same amount of food leads to an increase in bat mortality rates and a decrease in reproduction rates. Species that are not suited for long flights suffer most of all.

The effects of deforestation on the ecosystem

Deforestation affects the entire ecosystem in many ways. Because bats play such a key role in pollinating plants, the loss of bats in the rain forest—the 3.4 million

Leaf Tents for Bats

Some bats create their own roosting shelters by cutting leaves. Thomas Barbour, a scientist from Harvard University, described this process in 1932 while observing bats in Panama. He saw that a fruit-eating bat called the leaf-nosed bat (now called Peter's tent-making bat) used its claws to make certain kinds of cuts in newly emerged palm leaves. By folding the leaves, the bat built a sort of tent. During the 1980s other scientists found this same phenomenon in Costa Rica, Ecuador, and Peru.

Leaf-nosed bats, including the Caribbean white bat, are among those that build these leafy tents. The bats choose strong, waterproof leaves, such as anthuriums, palm fronds, and Panama hat palms, and the leaves stay alive after the bats alter their shapes and sizes.

The tent-building process takes a few days or longer. Some types of bats occupy their tents for several days, then move to a different tent they have built. Other types stay in the same tent for two or more months. A male fruit bat that lives in southern India may spend as much as two months fashioning a shelter from leaves and tree fronds. He then lives there with a harem of several female bats.

These tents shelter bats from rain, strong sunlight, and wind. They may also provide a safe place for newborn bats. Although mothers often carry their young with them when they forage for food, females of certain species may leave them alone in the tents some of the time.

square miles of tropical forest that encircle the equator—means that fewer seedlings will take root and grow into trees. This results in a vicious cycle: Less habitat means fewer bats, leading to less pollination and fewer new trees.

The loss of large trees also degrades the soil. When large trees are removed, the smaller patches of trees that remain are vulnerable to strong tropical storms. Topsoil is blown away or carried off by rainwater or flooding. This condition, called erosion, depletes the soil of valuable nutrients, without which canopy trees cannot germinate and grow. Mats of ground cover grow in these exposed areas instead, making it even harder for trees to take root.

With fewer trees, the soil becomes steadily poorer. There are fewer fruits, branches, and leaves on the ground to enrich the soil as they decay. Without these rich nutrients, trees and plants grow poorly, if at all, further depriving bats of food and habitats. Yet forest-dwelling bats are not the only species that are losing their habitats.

The loss of cave habitats

Bats have lost many of their cave roosting sites around the world because of natural disasters such as land slides and because of human activities that have become popular in recent times. For example, caves that were once quiet roosts are sometimes turned into tourist attractions or they attract cavers. Caving, known as spelunking, has become an increasingly popular form of recreation since the 1980s, and more people are exploring caves than ever before.

Spelunking, or cave exploration, has increased in popularity over the past two decades. Although a fascinating pursuit for people, it is an incursion into bat territory.

Even when these visitors are careful not to harm the bats, their movements and the noises they make can cause problems. Changes in the temperature or the airflow inside a cave or mine can be as devastating to bat colonies as the disturbances created by the visitors.

Humidity is also important. The Indiana bat, among other species, requires a hibernation site with high humidity. Seepage from watersheds located near caves makes their interiors humid enough for these bats to survive.

Some of the gates that have been put on cave entrances to restrict human access have also caused problems. To get through the openings on these gates, flying bats may have to slow down. Skunks, raccoons, and other predators can take advantage of slow-flying bats to attack them as they leave or enter the cave.

Numerous caves in the United States have become uninhabitable for bats. For example, since the early 1800s changes in the structure of Mammoth Cave in Kentucky led to the demise of millions of Indiana bats. During the War of 1812 miners discovered that the mine contained saltpeter, which was used to make gunpowder. In order to take oxen into the cave, they widened its interior passages and blocked certain entrances to make the cave warmer. A few years later, tourists began visiting Mammoth Cave and people enlarged the tunnels so that visitors could upright instead of crawling through the cave. Such intrusions, along with the changes in airflow, ruined this bat habitat, and they stopped roosting there.

Closing down some of the entrances of Mammoth Cave also upset the bats, since Indiana bats prefer caves with more than one entrance. Merlin D. Tuttle points out, "These bats can use less than 1 percent of caves, but these caves are the ones humans most like to explore."[12]

Certain bats live in just one or a few caves. For example, the hog-nosed bats of Thailand live in a limited area, and the Marinkelle's sword-nosed bat has only been found in one cave located in Colombia. These species are at greater risk of loss of habitat than others, and to survive, they may have to find and adapt to other habitats.

The loss of mine roosts

In places with few caves, mines provide bats with alternative roosting places. Mines offer a relatively stable temperature range, which the bats need to survive. They may use them as maternity roosts, as day and night roosts, and as places to hibernate in the winter. Some regions are riddled with these man-made bat lairs. For example, Nevada has at least three hundred thousand old mines.

Some species of bats live only in mines. An example is the Sanborn's long-nosed bat, which lives in the southwestern United States and northern Mexico. As of 2000,

A dinner party in Kentucky's Mammoth Cave in 1911. Intrusions here by tourists and miners eventually led to the loss of millions of Indiana bats.

two-thirds of the bat species in the United States were using abandoned mine shafts as roosting sites.

The destruction of abandoned mines has deprived many bats of their homes. Some old mines are destroyed to eliminate the dangers of cave-ins, poisonous gases, or aging, possibly unstable, explosives that have been stored inside. When dangerous portals are shut down in some mines,

Cave-roosting bats, such as these lesser long-nosed bats, may use abandoned mines as roosting sites in areas with few caves.

methane gases can build up to explosive levels and the bats will die unless they are carefully relocated. In North America, many mines have been blasted shut, barricaded, or backfilled in order to prevent accidents, which means that bats in these mines cannot leave, and bats that had lived there cannot return. In other places, open-pit mining operations have destroyed underground roosts.

Recent experiences in Australia's mines

Australia has few natural caves, and some of its rarest bats live in abandoned mines. A group of Troughton's sheath-tailed bats were killed when a mine shaft in Queensland was bulldozed. Bat conservationists worried that a species known as ghost bats, roosting in an old gold mine at Pine Creek in northern Australia, might also be killed after plans were made to conduct open-pit mining there. The plan was shelved when investigators found that the ore in the Pine Creek mine had little value.

However, ghost bats living in the caves of Mount Etna in Queensland have been declining since the 1960s as a result of limestone mining. These bats are rare, numbering only about three thousand. During the 1980s the Queensland National Parks and Wildlife Service completed a ten-year study which showed that at least two of Mount Etna's cave systems were vital for pregnant ghost bats. An article that appeared in the Summer 1989 issue of *Bats Magazine* discussed the reasons these roosts were so important:

> Speaking Tube Cave provides a warm over-wintering roost for all the pregnant females. The location of the cave, combined with its upward sloping chambers, creates the warmest winter cave conditions in the entire area, and large open flyways inside the cave make roost access easy for heavily pregnant females. Ghost bats cannot lower their body temperature and they do not cluster, so they must find roost sites with temperatures above 68 Fahrenheit. Below this temperature, they have to shiver to keep warm. Speaking Tube Cave is one of the few caves which remain above 68 during the winter.[13]

In addition to ghost bats, sheath-tailed bats, horseshoe bats, and two species of bent-wing bats live in these caves.

All five of these species now have protected status under the country's Fauna Preservation Act.

Bat Cleft Cave, part of Mount Etna, provides maternity roosts for about 80 percent of the total bat population in that region. Conservationists have opposed activities that endanger the bats and have urged mining companies to extract limestone from other sources, where mining would not have such a profound impact on the environment. However, in 1988 a cement-making company was permitted to destroy parts of Speaking Tube Cave and Elephant Hole Cave, leaving piles of rubble in the entrances of these two caves. In 1989 Speaking Tube Cave was blasted and destroyed. Although parts of the Mount Etna area have been set aside as a reserve and a national park, limestone mining continues outside the protected area.

During the late 1990s about ten thousand common bent-wing, little bent-wing and eastern horseshoe bats were living in an inactivated mine in Queensland. For safety reasons, some of the portals were closed and ventilation was shut down, leading to an intense buildup of methane gases. Conservation organizations helped the Queensland National Parks and Wildlife Service relocate these bats in an artificial mine habitat.

As mines disappear, some bats find new habitats

The number of mines throughout the world continues to decline. Sometimes mines are destroyed before people realize that bats are roosting inside. Some states and countries have passed laws that require people to inspect mines for bats before destroying the sites. Some mine owners are also becoming more interested in the fate of bats that live on their property.

To survive, some bats who must leave mines or other habitats discover new ones. Some species are willing to roost in new places, such as roof voids, attics, vacant buildings, and barns, if their natural roosts are destroyed. Such attempts to adapt to new surroundings can help them to survive; but, if they choose dangerous places, they will die as surely as if they had stayed in a methane-filled mine.

By studying the movements of radio-tagged bats, scientists have found that certain bats in the Golan Heights region of Israel will roost in abandoned military bunkers. African and Egyptian bats have been tracked from hollow trees to water towers to old military bunkers. Scientists hope that ongoing studies will help them find ways to help bats make these kinds of changes.

4

Rescue Efforts

SINCE THE 1970s increasing numbers of people have been working at the local, national, regional, and international levels to protect endangered bats and their habitats. Governments, large and small organizations, academic institutions, charitable foundations, and individuals are all part of this effort, and they often form partnerships.

Bat conservationists are involved in many kinds of projects and activities around the world. They engage in research and public education and take direct action to rescue individual bats and entire colonies or species. Some organizations lobby for stricter laws and enforcement and file lawsuits to protect bats and their habitats.

International treaties

Governments around the world have taken cooperative action to save bats and their habitats.

The Convention on International Trade in Endangered Species of Wild Fauna and Flora (CITES) is the most far-reaching international agreement. CITES was ratified in 1975 by 96 nations, including the United States, and now has a membership of 144 countries. CITES, which maintains a list of endangered species, affects a wide range of plants and animals and makes it a crime to sell or transport an endangered species or any products made from these species. Among other things, this treaty restricts international trade in fruit bats in many Pacific islands.

In Europe, the European Bats Agreement (1992) and the European Union Habitats and Species Directive (1992) address the preservation of foraging habitats. In the action plan that was enacted in accordance with the European Bats Agreement, in 1995 parties agreed to what authors Thomas H. Kunz and Paul A. Racey call

> a wide-ranging conservation and management plan, which involves survey and monitoring of populations, the identification and protection of important roosts and foraging habitats, and the promotion of public awareness about bats.[14]

National laws

Individual nations also have laws that protect bats and their habitats. An example is the U.S. Endangered Species Act, which Congress passed in 1973. The act aims to conserve the ecosystems on which endangered species depend and to discourage the destruction of these species around the world. The act states that endangered species may not be "killed, hunted, collected, harassed, harmed, pursued, shot, trapped, wounded, or captured."[15]

Numerous other countries have their own special protective laws as well. In Germany, laws protect all of the twenty-two

An intern from Bat Conservation International gives a presentation to elementary school children.

The Bat Rescue Team in Africa

A group of concerned citizens in South Africa recently joined together to form the Bat Action Team, also called Cape BAT. The members include representatives of the Speleological Society (cave enthusiasts), the Endangered Wildlife Trust, and Cape Nature Conservation. Hundreds of different bat species live in this region, and they play key roles in pollination and pest control.

One of Cape BAT's first projects was to compile a bat atlas in order to gather information about the different bats and their needs. It also designated a bat expert whom people could contact to advise homeowners who found bats in their homes. The group hopes this will prevent people from poisoning bats, which is illegal in South Africa. In addition, Cape BAT began urging people to put up bat houses to provide additional or alternative roosts.

In the article "Bat Action Team Rallies to Rescue Cape Bat," which appeared in a newsletter of the University of Cape Town, David Jacobs, a professor of zoology at the university, states:

> Even with our rich diversity of over 900 species, conservation of bats in the Cape is long overdue. . . . Cape BAT's conservation efforts will thus focus on the prevention of bat habitat loss as well as the protection of roosts, the prevention of poisoning and on education and research.

species of bats that live there. In Great Britain, the Wildlife and Countryside Act (1981) bans killing any bat. Of the sixteen species of bats that still live in Great Britain, six are endangered or rare, and six others are considered vulnerable. The mouse-eared bat was declared extinct from Britain in 1991. In Canada, the British Columbia Provincial Wildlife Acts protects bats and requires people to obtain a special permit to kill a bat.

Some laws address specific threats to bat survival, such as hunting. In the U.S. Commonwealth of the Northern Mariana Islands, for instance, laws restrict the hunting of fruit bats, some of which are critically endangered. In 1983 the commonwealth issued Public Law 2-51, which states, in part,

It shall be unlawful to take fruit bats on the islands of Rota, Tinian, Aguiguan, and Saipan for a period of two years from the effective date of these regulations. Further it shall be unlawful to take fruit bats on any island north of Saipan for a period of one year.[16]

Voluntary efforts to protect bats

Interestingly, in some supposedly primitive places, people appreciate and protect their bats. On the South Pacific island of Tonatabu, for example, the Tongan fruit bat is considered to be sacred, and hunting it is forbidden. This social norm protects bats from human predation.

In Samoa, a three-year ban on hunting bats was enacted in 1992. The law banned people from selling or bartering bats or hunting them in the daytime. Bats could be hunted only in May, June, and July, and each hunter was limited to seven bats per day.

However, critics say these laws are not always enforced. Some countries cannot spare the money to fund patrols in

A young poacher in Southeast Asia removes a bat from a net. Although laws protecting bats have been enacted, they are not always enforced.

all of the areas where bats live, and few people have the time or the inclination to volunteer for this task. A single patrolman might be in charge of a large region, and, in some cases, there are no jails in which to put offenders. In addition, conservation laws have failed because they protected only the animals themselves, not the critical roosts and habitats.

Countries have also created national bat conservation plans. Examples include the Australian Bat Action Plan and federal bat conservation units in Brazil. Some countries, such as Slovakia, are developing comprehensive bat protective programs for the first time. Conservationists in Slovakia have received help from Bat Conservation International, an organization that assists people who lack enough resources to carry out bat research and conservation programs.

In October 1999 Australia's federal environment minister, Robert Hill, said that their action plan aims to provide a national overview of the conservation of the ninety species that live in Australia. Recommendations in the plan include research to find out more about the status of little-known species, habitat preservation, installing gates at roost entrances, and setting up a national bat expert panel to advise the government on how to implement the plan.

The Australian plan is important because conservationists have expressed special concern about Australia, claiming that half of the mammalian extinctions in the world have occurred in that country during the past two hundred years. As of 2000, eighty-five bat species in Australia were classified as threatened by the International Union for the Conservation of Nature and Natural Resources. The major threat to Australian bats is the loss of forest and mine habitats.

Organizations

A number of nonprofit organizations work on behalf of bats. As the twenty-first century began, these kinds of organizations were growing and working in more countries than ever before. Some of them, such as the World Wildlife Federation and Earthjustice (a division of the Sierra Club),

Appealing Pictures

Merlin D. Tuttle began photographing bats in 1978 when the National Geographic Society asked him to write a chapter about bats for a book it was creating.

Through the years Tuttle has sometimes faced danger and has often spent days studying a particular bat or group of bats in order to get the right photo at the right time. In an article that appeared in the Winter 1988 issue of *Bats Magazine*, Tuttle recalled one of his adventures while photographing bats in a jungle in Thailand. It was late at night and Tuttle's group had spotted tigers in the area. He was waiting alone with his nets, hoping an armed guard might show up before the tigers.

In that same article, Tuttle described another trip, this time to Guam, when he climbed a hundred feet up a tree that was swaying in the wind in order to take a picture of a Mariana fruit bat. He says, "Climbing tall jungle trees at night to build a set is hardly for the faint of heart, but . . . some pictures can be taken only in the wild." When he takes pictures inside a studio, Tuttle says, "My bats are harmlessly netted, gently handled and released as quickly as possible."

In an article titled "Bracken Cave Near San Antonio," author Patrick Beach quotes Tuttle as saying, "I had to be rescued by the Venezuelan army from communist guerrillas, I've had my camp shot up, I've met cobras. . . . I've had plenty of excitement."

address a broad range of issues and species; other groups, however, focus on one particular concern, such as bats.

Bat Conservation International (BCI) is a well-known organization devoted to bat research, education, and conservation. BCI has more than fourteen thousand members in sixty countries and employs more than thirty biologists, educators, and administrators. BCI encourages people to collaborate in order to balance the needs of humans and wildlife and to find positive solutions that benefit people as well as animals and the environment.

Through its efforts, many of the world's largest remaining bat populations have been granted permanent legal protection. The organization has also educated many people about bats and has improved the animals' public image. It has trained hundreds of leading wildlife managers who work in agencies throughout the world. BCI also buys caves so that it can control what goes on around them. For example, it owns Bracken Cave in San Antonio, Texas, the cave that holds the largest colony of mammals on the earth, about 40 million Mexican free-tailed bats.

The Organization for Bat Conservation (OBC) is another nonprofit organization that aims to protect bats and their habitats. Founded in 1991, the OBC works throughout the United States to educate people about bats, conduct research, and work with people on specific projects that help bats. Educational programs are presented at schools, zoos, parks, museums, nature centers, and clubs. The organization also carries out projects that enable bats to receive proper veterinary care.

The International Union for the Conservation of Nature and Natural Resources (IUCN) was founded in 1948. By 2000, it had grown to more than 880 member states, government agencies, and nongovernmental organizations from 133 countries. One of the IUCN's departments, the Species Survival Commission, includes a subdivision called the Chiropteran Specialist Group, which concentrates on bats.

One of the organizations that helped to create the IUCN is Fauna and Flora International (FFI), the world's oldest international conservation group. FFI works to safeguard endangered species of plants and animals and played a key role in the creation of CITES.

Several organizations work on behalf of bats in Britain. The Bat Conservation Trust (BCT) is the largest of these and the only organization in the United Kingdom whose sole purpose is conserving bats and their habitats. The BCT carries out conservation projects and research, educates people about bats, and helps those who find bats on their property to preserve their roosts. The Norfolk Bat

Group and the Staffordshire Bat Group are among the many regional groups devoted to bat preservation.

Studying bats

Research is a key part of efforts to save bats. Although scientists now know more about bats than they did thirty years ago, bats as a group remain among the least understood

Scientists catch a Kitti's hog-nosed bat in a mist net.

animals in the world. In some cases, scientists have gathered solid information about a certain aspect of a species' life, such as its winter roosting habits, but they still do not understand other aspects, such as feeding.

A lack of funding has limited bat research projects. Faced with immediate pressures to provide for the welfare and defense of citizens, few governments are able to spare the money to sponsor extensive research on bats, examining their habitats, foraging habits, and other parts of their life history. Nonprofit organizations have taken a leading role in these efforts, and BCI has been the most active organization studying bats around the world.

Private industry has also contributed funds for bat conservation research. In 1999 British Petroleum provided a twenty-thousand-dollar grant to assist the Madagascar Bat Project 2000. The true status of bat populations in Madagascar, one of the world's poorest countries, is unknown. Certain rare species, such as the sucker-footed bat, live there. Scientists working on this project will be using methods that enable them to identify bats by listening to their calls instead of physically capturing them.

In England, the BCT conducted the National Bats in Churches Survey between 1992 and 1994. It showed that 90 percent of the 132 churches used as roosting sites in the late 1960s were still occupied by bats in the 1990s. The study also showed that bats generally occupied buildings that were surrounded by pre-1800 buildings and avoided those in neighborhoods that had been modernized.

Bat research: goals and hopes

As they look for ways to save endangered bats, conservationists study bats and their habitats and analyze certain risk factors as they apply to different species of bats: small numbers, rarity, population declines, limited distribution, restricted habitat requirements, limited diets, foraging habits, hibernating requirements, and special vulnerability to human actions. Scientists also study bat populations to

see the rate of growth and the number of young produced each year.

Researchers want to learn enough about bats' living habits to understand how various threats will affect them; once this is determined, researchers can then attempt to minimize or eliminate those threats. In some cases, researchers tag and mark bats inhabiting caves, bat boxes attached to trees, or other places, and then study them for a period of months and years. Recent studies are providing this kind of information. Radio-tracking studies have

Scientists take a bat census to aid in their research.

shown that bats usually forage within four kilometers of their roost.

Scientists also examine why bats seem to favor certain types of landscapes. For reasons that are not yet understood, bats tend to prefer places that are not too brightly lit or open, perhaps because there is more risk from predation in more exposed areas. Species differ in regard to the types of landscapes they choose.

Scientists also want to know how some bats move from one type of habitat to another. In Europe and North America, for example, people have been finding out more about how far from their roosts bats hunt for food. They have studied the kinds of new roosts bats develop after old roosting places are destroyed. Some studies in Europe focus on the lesser horseshoe bat, which typically roosted in caves year-round. However, these bats have recently adopted buildings for their summer roosts. Through such research, scientists hope to discover effective ways to help bats adapt to new surroundings.

Protecting cave habitats

Bat conservationists focus much time and money on protecting bats' habitats, especially the habitats of endangered species. To prevent vandalism in caves, for instance, individuals and groups have taken direct action by erecting gates.

Responding to the 1998 killing of forty bats at Wolf River Cave in Tennessee, the Nature Conservancy proposed that a ten-thousand-pound gate be placed at the entrance. The gate was constructed in such a way that bats could still get in and out. People would not be allowed to enter during the bats' winter hibernating period, and during the spring and summer, the local caving club and the cave owner would control access.

The organization was working with the cave's landowner, the U.S. Fish and Wildlife Service, the American Cave Conservation Association, and other organizations to complete this project. Speaking for the Nature Conservancy, Gabrielle Call says, "This cave came to the forefront because of its Indiana bats and the recent vandalism."[17] Call points out that this cave was home to Tennessee's second largest population of Indiana bats (about 2,550) and that this species was still on the decline. According to Call, "At this rate, they'll be extinct in 12 years."[18]

The Hubbard's Cave gating project in Tennessee is designed to control human access to caves.

Protecting mine habitats

To protect bats in abandoned mines, conservationists say that a biological survey should be conducted before a mine is destroyed. Instead of blasting mines with explosives, they recommend that gates be installed with gratings that let bats pass through but block humans. Gates are more expensive, however, and this method requires more time than simply blowing up an unproductive mine. The cost of the gates themselves may range from several hundred dollars to thousands.

Nonetheless, this method is becoming more popular. The staff at the Great Basin National Park tries to make abandoned mines safer while still protecting bats. They check the mines to see if bats are inhabiting them. If so, they install barriers that protect both humans and bats. The Townsend's big-eared bat and the big free-tailed bat are among the bat species that live within the park's limits.

The U.S. Fish and Wildlife Service, concerned about bats in all underground habitats, has worked to acquire and manage caves in which Indiana bats hibernate during the winter. As of 2000, the government owned or controlled 54 of the 127 caves and mines with populations of more than 100 bats. Forty-six of the 127 caves had been gated or fenced to protect bat populations. However, because some bats do not like to fly between metal bars or through small holes, metal gates have posed problems for bats living in caves or mines. So, in some cases concrete has been used instead. An opening large enough for the bats to pass through is made near the top of the concrete barrier.

The North American Bats and Mines Project (NABMP) is another example of a concerted effort. In 1994 the NABMP was founded to protect mine-roosting bat populations threatened by mine closures and reclamations. The organization pointed out that more than 50 percent of U.S. bat species use abandoned mines and these bats eat great quantities of insects that farmers and foresters spend billions of dollars each year trying to control.

The NABMP has worked with state agencies, private foundations, universities, and other bat conservation organizations to protect mine-roosting bats. It has worked especially hard in Michigan, Wisconsin, and Minnesota.

From outcasts to tourist attraction

People who once wanted bats out of their area have sometimes changed their minds. In 1980 repairs were being made to the Congress Avenue Bridge, which spans Town Lake in downtown Austin, Texas. Although for many years a small number of bats had lived under the bridge, the new construction created crevices the right size for roosting sites and for raising young bats. As a result, more than a million Mexican free-tailed bats, mostly females, were attracted to the bridge.

At first people were frightened by this huge colony and asked the government to get rid of the bats. However, the bridge began to attract sightseers who wanted to observe the bats, which make up the largest urban colony in North America. Bat supporters pointed out the advantages of having so many insect-eating bats in the area. Now the Congress Avenue Bridge is a tourist attraction and people visit to watch the stream of bats emerge on their nightly foraging trips. Bat Conservation International (BCI) and the Austin Parks and Recreation Department set up an educational kiosk on the north bank of the river near the bridge to inform people about the bats and their history.

The bats roost at the bridge between mid-March and early November, and during those months, they eat tens of thousands of pounds of insects every night. During the winter, they live in central Mexico.

In recent years, more bats are being welcomed on bridges in other places, too. Conservationists have urged companies to build new bridges in such a way that bats will find places to roost and congregate there.

Involved citizens

Numerous people around the world have donated their time to bat conservation. They have worked as individuals

Bat flight from the Congress Avenue Bridge in Austin, Texas. Tourists often visit the Bridge to observe bat activity.

or with groups to carry out projects that will help bats and their habitats survive.

A number of bat conservationists rescue and care for displaced or orphaned bats, and others help homeowners to humanely evict bats from their homes. Some work at bat hospitals and rehabilitation centers. Michele Chubb, who raises orphaned bats in her home near Brisbane, Australia, says, "Each one has a distinct personality, but they all return your affection ten-fold. They are like kids: curious, responsive, always into mischief."[19]

Volunteers frequently inspect mines that are scheduled for demolition. They look for bat colonies and report these findings to the authorities, who then decide how to deal with the mine in order to preserve the bats' roosts.

Other people help to construct cave gates. In West Virginia volunteers have built large, sturdy gates at the entrances of caves that were easily accessible to the public. In 1999 over forty people helped to build a gate at Schoolhouse Cave in Germany Valley to protect Virginia big-eared bats, which are on the endangered list. In 2000, volunteers put up gates at Hoffman School Cave and Minor Rexrode Cave, both located in Pendleton County. They worked with the state's Division of Natural Resources Non-Game Wildlife and Natural Heritage Program, the Canaan Valley National Wildlife Refuge, and the American Cave Conservation Association on these projects.

Bats in zoos and captive-breeding programs

Zoos, too, are playing a much more active role in preserving bat species. Many zoos, especially in North America, have been promoting public education, research, and conservation.

Exhibits are now designed to give bats more flying space and room to turn around. For example, in 1991 the Metro Washington Zoo in Portland, Oregon, included a bat display in its African rain forest exhibit. One hundred fruit bats of four different species live in the ten-foot-tall, sixty-six-foot-long enclosure.

Visitors to Jungleworld, a large aviary-style exhibit at the Wildlife Conservation Park/Bronx Zoo in New York City, can see Indiana fruit bats, reptiles, monkeys, and many kinds of birds. The exhibit, which was built in 1985, covers about 1 million square feet. Zookeeper Peter Riger says, "People are taken aback when they see the bats hanging there, not separated from visitors by anything. But I've never heard any negative comments about the bats; people think they're pretty neat."[20]

Bats are being bred in captivity in zoos and private collections in the United States, Europe, the Philippines, and other places. Captive-breeding programs aim to increase the number of bats whose survival is in doubt. Examples of bats being bred in captivity are the

 Rodrigues Bats in Captivity

The Jersey Zoo, located in the Channel Islands off the coast of England, has taken an active part in captive breeding. In 1976 the Jersey Wildlife Preservation Trust (JWPT) worked with staff at the zoo to capture some Rodrigues fruit bats from Mauritius and develop two captive populations. Other colonies were founded in the United States and England. As of 1991, 250 of these bats were in captivity. Another captive colony, this time with Livingstone's fruit bats, was established at this zoo during the 1990s. This was no easy task. According to Janette Young of the JWPT, who was quoted in the Wildlife Trust's on-line article "Livingstone's Fruit Bat," this species is "one of the largest of the world's fruit bats, certainly the rarest, undoubtedly the most stunning, and absolutely the most difficult to capture."

Several fruit bats have been born at the zoo. A baby born in December 1996 was rejected by its mother. The staff, who named the fruit bat "Merlin," raised it. One of the zookeepers kept it in his bedroom, fed it, and patiently encouraged it to fly. Merlin grew to adulthood and was living in the bat habitat at the zoo in 2000. Bananas are one of his favorite foods. All of the bats in the zoo have a diet featuring pineapple, papaya, thinned applesauce, figs, and avocado.

Rodrigues flying fox, Livingstone's fruit bat, and the Mariana fruit bat. The ultimate goal of many breeding programs is to return animals to the wild when they are more numerous and their natural habitat is restored and protected.

5

What Lies Ahead?

As of 2000, dozens of species of bats were endangered throughout the world and on every continent they inhabit. Conservationists say that early intervention is often necessary if a species is to survive, especially in the case of bats, since small colonies have lower rates of survival. Experts note that many of today's endangered species were common just twenty or thirty years ago.

Yet some bats try hard to adapt. Certain species have found ways to benefit from human activity by exploiting new feeding opportunities. Author M. Brock Fenton describes some of them:

> One of the most obvious of these is the tendency of vampire bats to feed on the blood of cattle and other domestic animals.
> . . . In southern England, serotines [large insect-eating bats common in Great Britain] often feed over new-mown fields, while greater horseshoe bats hunt dung beetles associated with cattle. In Germany, radio-tagged noctules [also large insect-eating bats] often hunted over dumps, exploiting the insects attracted there. Almost everywhere, many insectivorous bats hunt in the clouds of insects attracted to streetlights.[21]

Hard choices for a crowded planet

Habitat destruction remains the greatest threat to bats, but laws to control it may be hard to enforce. Nations with limited resources often rely on forest products to provide income, fuel, and building materials. As the earth becomes more and more crowded, the demand for resources, including land, water, food, and energy, will continue to grow.

At times, efforts to help endangered animals, including bats, conflict with business interests and property rights. For example, mining and timber companies don't want to sacrifice profits for habitat protection. However, many companies are beginning to recognize the benefits to be gained by protecting bat habitat. Protection of preferred trees used by bats as roosts can benefit the timber industry because bats eat timber pests such as bark beetles. Gates on abandoned mines allow bats to enter, but keep people out, thereby protecting mining companies from liability issues that result when people enter old mine shafts.

Furthermore, conservation programs that help some species may have a negative impact on others. For instance,

A little brown bat shows its fangs.

In parts of Africa the increase in elephant populations has led to their moving into and devastating various bat habitats.

in parts of Africa where people have worked to increase elephant populations, these animals have moved into areas where bats live. According to surveys conducted in 1997, the bats, along with birds, tended to die or move out of these places. In some parts of Zimbabwe, elephant populations have been increasing by about 5 percent a year—about the same rate as human populations. Woodlands in some national parks, such as Matusadona, and other protected areas in Africa have been devastated by the increasing number of elephants.

The Return of an Ice Age Bat

Occasionally a bat that is considered extinct will reappear. This happened with the world's largest bat: the endangered Bulmer's fruit bat, which has been around since the Ice Age. It was twice considered extinct, only to be rediscovered. This amazing large bat, which can fly backward and can also hover in the air, was thought to have died out ten thousand years ago until people sighted it in New Guinea during the 1970s.

The tribe of New Guineans who lived near a cave of Bulmer's fruit bats regarded them as sacred, and their traditions banned killing the bats. However, some intruders from another tribe entered the cave where the bats lived and shot them for food during the 1970s. The bats seemed to have died out until a few of them were spotted in that same cave in 1992.

People around the world face decisions that will affect the status of wildlife and their habitats. These choices have both short-term and long-term consequences. Some efforts to help bats call for time, money, and other resources and require people to make sacrifices or trade-offs; meanwhile, others are relatively simple and inexpensive.

Public education as a means of helping bats

Educating people about the importance of bats remains a key goal for lasting progress in conserving these animals and their habitats. In many countries nonprofit conservation groups are doing more for this effort than the government. These organizations continue to help people understand the need to protect bats and to operate citizen training programs, to offer practical solutions for local problems, and to train educators and wildlife managers who will carry on this work in regions throughout the world.

For example, during 1998 Bat Conservation International (BCI) held several Bat Educator Workshops that were attended by hundreds of teachers and park interpreters. During these workshops, BCI presented the most up-to-date methods and tools for teaching people about bats. BCI also continues to create videos and other multimedia tools for educators, and it provides scholarship money for graduate students from many countries so that they can study the ecological and economic roles and conservation needs of bats.

Meanwhile, other bat advocates the world over are working to change negative and indifferent attitudes. They try to reduce fears and encourage people not to harm or disturb bats and to support measures that save bats' habitats and roosting areas. Education programs seek to show people exactly how bats help them, their economy, and the entire earth. For example, BCI has worked in Southeast Asia to publicize its findings that more than 450 commercial products in that region depend on bats, mostly fruit bats that pollinate plants.

Public education is regarded as an essential part of conservation efforts. South American naturalist Luis F. Aguirre says, "If we are able to reach young people . . . , we know there is hope for the bats of Bolivia."[22]

Changing attitudes

Although thanks largely to the dedicated efforts of conservationists bats generally received favorable attention in the last decades of the twentieth century, they remain unpopular in some places. In South and Central America, people still kill bats because they fear infected vampire bats threaten livestock and people. According to zoologist and bat expert John D. Altringham,

> Vaccination programmes have led to a much lower incidence of rabies in domestic livestock, but it still remains a problem. Rabies infection of humans by vampires was once relatively high in some parts of the New World, but cases are increasingly rare due to improved public health.[23]

Authors Jader Marinho-Filho and Ivan Sazima write:

> in Brazil [bats] are seen by common people as vermin or even as harmful creatures associated with blood-feeding vampires. Possibly because of this poor public image, bats have been largely neglected in conservation and environmental education programs in Brazil and elsewhere in South America.[24]

These authors conclude, "It is clear that direct measures to counteract the loss of Brazilian bat diversity are unlikely to be realized in the short term." They say that protecting native areas will probably be "more productive and cost-effective than species oriented strategies."[25]

Aguirre writes about the problems bats face in Bolivia, saying they are

> probably the most misunderstood animals in my country. In some areas, young boys mistakenly hunt them for display in their insect collections. In other places, people have so little regard for bats—which they see as dirty, ugly, rabid and portents of bad luck—that they participate in a depraved pastime of catching small bats and making them "smoke" cigarettes.

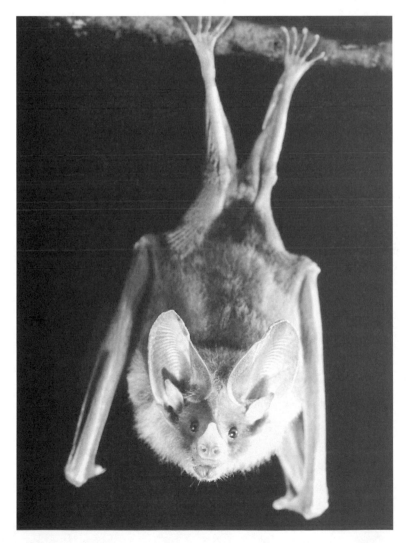

Many people find it difficult to feel sympathy and understanding for bats.

This malicious attitude . . . added to the significant problem of vampire bats feeding on cattle, has led ranchers and other citizens to conduct campaigns in which they burn known roost sites and kill every bat they encounter, regardless of species.[26]

Conflicts over logging

Many ongoing debates over endangered species concern economics. Loggers depend on the income they earn by cutting down trees in forests where bats and other animals live. In some countries, logging is one of the primary industries. Debates over logging of native forests are often heated, and the forest industry may fight efforts to stop them from logging in certain areas.

In 1998 environmentalists took legal action to suspend logging in an area of the Allegheny National Forest in northwestern Pennsylvania after an adult male Indiana bat was found there in August. Indiana bats prefer large trees, including dead or dying trees, with loose bark.

Members of Heartwood, Inc., a company based in Indiana that sells and repairs doors for homeowners and businesses, and the Allegheny Defense Project sought to stop sixty-one logging operations in the 510,000-acre forest. Their attorney, William Luneberg, stated at the time,

Studies show that endangered bats are very loyal and if the habitat is destroyed in areas where they are known to live, the bats will die. Plus, continued cutting reduces usable habitat and could very well interfere with the future recovery of the species.[27]

As it considered the interests of the parties involved, the U.S. Forest Service ruled that tree cutting on existing contracts could continue. It observed the loggers at work to ensure that they were not disturbing bats.

Conservation efforts stave off habitat destruction

To combat tree loss, reforestation projects are increasing around the world. The government of Australia announced a plan to reforest twenty-five thousand hectares (ten thousand acres) of land per year. Critics say that is still less than the current annual rate of habitat destruction. Australia has

The economic interests of the logging industry are often at odds with the goals of bat conservationists.

often been criticized for the large-scale habitat destruction that has taken place there since Europeans arrived.

Some land is cleared to make way for new crop-growing areas. In some places, farmers move from plot to plot after they deplete the soil in each area. Conservationists teach these people ways to enrich the soil so they need not continue to clear new ground.

In 2000, scientists declared that about half of the world's mangrove swamps had been destroyed. In some parts of Asia and Central and South America, people are clearing them to make room for the commercial cultivation of shrimp. This practice makes the former swampland vulnerable to serious tropical storm damage, however, and governments are mounting educational programs to persuade shrimp farmers to set up their farms farther inland. Water for the shrimp ponds could be transported by pipes and canals, leaving the mangroves intact.

Australian farmers maintain that fruit bats such as this flying fox cost them millions of dollars in fruit loss. Other analysts say that these figures are exaggerated.

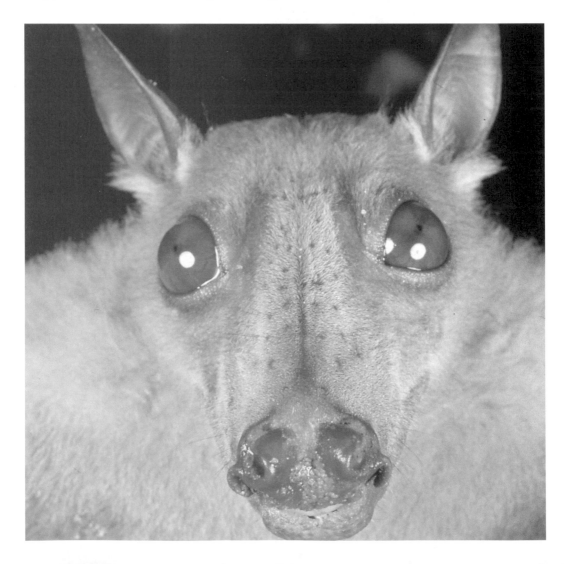

Conservation efforts and the cost to farmers

What about the cost to orchard owners when fruit bats are allowed to roam freely? Australian farmers still regard flying foxes as pests, and it has been estimated that they cause about $20 million worth of damage each year to the commercial fruit industry. Other analysts say fruit growers have exaggerated these figures. According to Altringham,

> Damage to fruit crops by bats can be severe but even this is generally overestimated. When costs have been assessed objectively they are frequently low and must be offset against the positive gains of improved pollination success.[28]

Other researchers point out that bats rarely eat fruits that are destined for export because these fruits are picked when they are slightly unripe so that they can be shipped without rotting. Bats are most likely to eat fruits that ripen after the main crop has been harvested. This can actually benefit the grower since it reduces the chance of mold and crop pests such as fruit flies.

In cases in which bats do extensive damage, some local governments have enacted laws that take both sides into account. For example, in New Caledonia, part of the Cook Islands of the South Pacific, bats hurt coconut palm plantations. People are permitted to hunt bats from April to the end of June, but not at other times. The limit is ten bats per hunter per day, and to remove the profit motive, people are banned from marketing bats at all times.

Conservationists find support from many sources

In some cases, conservationists also help hunters and farmers find alternatives. For instance, nets can be used to keep bats out of orchards without killing them and they also keep out birds and prevent hail from damaging crops. Although the netting requires an initial investment, the cost is recovered in a few years.

In 1986 John Gough, who raises peaches and nectarines in northern New South Wales, Australia, developed a type of exclusion netting and installed it over all ten acres of his orchard. Gough, who is also a conservationist, has urged farmers to plant more trees to replace bat habitat. He says,

"Before the habitat can be restored, nets provide the best insurance against the bats. You can buy yourself many nights of stress-free sleep, which is priceless."[29] Since 1997 Gough's netting company has seen a surge in orders. That year the eucalyptus trees did not blossom, and farmers reported higher crop losses as forest bats foraged in orchards.

In places where people depend on bats as a source of protein in their diets, conservationists look for other foods to replace them. Some governments also compensate people who suffer economic losses when they permit bats to use their property.

Other conflicts arise when bats live near the site of proposed development. In 1999 people in Pennsylvania began debating whether to complete a $450 million interstate highway project. Indiana bats hibernate at a limestone cave near the proposed highway. Scientists estimate that about two hundred to three hundred of these bats, half the total living in Pennsylvania, winter in this cave. They fear the projected highway will threaten the bats' survival by frightening them away from roosting areas. After over a year of discussion, no decision had been made.

The tools and goals of new research

Ongoing research is addressing questions about the roosting habits of endangered bats. New instruments make it possible for researchers to count bats more accurately and to study their behavior. For example, scientists are finding ways to locate and count bats by the sounds they make so that they do not have to physically capture or handle the animals. Such new information will also be used to plan conservation efforts.

The Organization for Bat Conservation has been carrying out projects that provide crucial information about bats' habitats. In some studies, it stretches mist nets across a body of water and catches bats foraging for insects. The organization carefully removes, identifies, weighs, and describes the bats, then attaches tiny radio transmitters to their bodies in order to follow their activities. Such track-

Humane Evictions

Each year many bats are displaced for various reasons. Some move into homes and other buildings where they are unwelcome. People who find bats in their attics or walls may want to get rid of them.

A number of organizations, including Bat Conservation International, the Organization for Bat Conservation, and the California Bat Conservation Fund, help displaced bats through humane evictions. Bat experts point out that bats can be evicted during the early spring and late fall, but they should not be evicted during nursery season—early May through September—because baby bats cannot fly out with their mothers.

A safe way to evict bats is by fastening netting over the openings through which they enter a house; however, this must be done in such a way that the bats are still able to crawl out of the house but cannot get back in. People can also put up bat houses or boxes to replace their roosting places.

Urban Wildlife Rescue, Inc., rescues displaced bats in Colorado. One such rescue in October 2000 involved a silverhair bat that had been roosting on the outside wall of a business. The man who had called the group about the bat had named it Pombo and had persuaded his coworkers not to harm it.

In Urban Wildlife Rescue's on-line article "Pombo the Bat," the rescuers say,

> Pombo is one of the smartest, most docile bats we have offered haven to. He ate all of the bugs out of his dish right away and never threatened to bite us. He will be released in the spring in the same area where we found him and, hopefully, he will find a friendlier place to sleep.

ing devices enable researchers to learn where bats roost, what types of habitat they prefer, how close to humans they will roost, and how much habitat they need.

In 1999 Merlin D. Tuttle and Jim Kennedy, researchers from Bat Conservation International, studied the hibernation needs of Indiana bats living in caves in Kentucky, Tennessee, Missouri, Indiana, and Illinois. They analyzed whether the temperature, humidity, and other conditions in caves favor the long-term survival of this species.

In the course of this study, Tuttle and Kennedy found ways to improve cave and mine conditions for bats. They write:

> We have recommended a variety of specific and relatively simple actions that, in our opinion, could prove extremely beneficial to

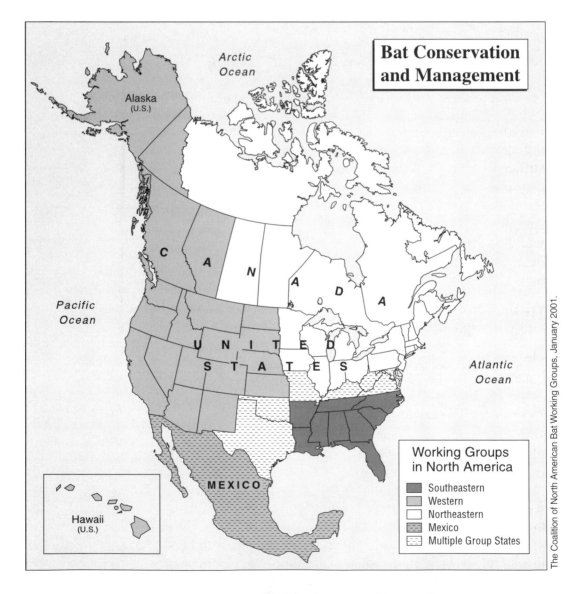

Bat Conservation and Management

Working Groups in North America

- Southeastern
- Western
- Northeastern
- Mexico
- Multiple Group States

The Coalition of North American Bat Working Groups, January 2001.

Indiana bat recovery. . . . Most of the improvements we have suggested would not be either expensive or highly inconvenient.[30]

They suggested eliminating openings that adversely affect the temperature inside. Other caves needed more openings for bats to come and go. In places where caves were weak, walls could be fortified to prevent cave-ins.

Ongoing research is considered essential in order to save this species. Despite concerted efforts to protect the hibernation sites and maternity roosts of Indiana bats, the species is not recovering at a sufficient rate. Scientists believe they will have to learn more about the bats' summer ecology and summer habitat requirements, as well as their migration patterns, to determine how to help Indiana bats survive.

Human-made roosts

As natural roosts decline, people are providing more artificial bat shelters than ever before. Building bat boxes or houses is a relatively simple and inexpensive way to provide new roosting sites and to increase bat populations. These boxes, which are gaining fans in the United States, have been popular in Europe since the 1930s. The houses are wooden and include slats inside for roosting.

Bat Conservation International developed its North American Bat House Research Project to provide more housing for bats. Local nature centers and state agencies also provide information that helps people put up these boxes. Thousands of people have erected them in their

This man-made bat condominium is intended to provide a home for bats whose natural roosts are becoming scarce.

yards or neighborhoods, and some voluntarily record the bat activity they observe.

Bat houses are especially helpful in places with few natural roosting places. In England people have put up thousands of bat boxes in the past twenty years. These boxes are placed in forests where trees are relatively new and do not provide the cracks, loose bark, woodpecker holes, and other kinds of cavities that many bats prefer.

Studies show that the majority of bats using bat houses are groups of mothers who need a nursery, but they also serve as summer homes for single male bats. Certain types of bats, especially little brown bats, big brown bats, the eastern pipestrelle, and the eastern long-eared bat, will use bat boxes as places to roost, hibernate, and raise their young. These species were not endangered or threatened as of 2000.

Improving human-made bat roosts

Researchers are looking for ways to make bat houses serve bats year-round. Recent studies show that bats prefer certain house designs; for instance, large colony houses with an extended area below them have higher occupancy rates.

Bat expert Altringham writes,

> Clearly bat boxes are fulfilling many useful roles. They are a valuable field laboratory for bat research, much of it conservation-oriented. They also are an important public relations vehicle, attracting the attention of the community and the media. Finally, they are heavily used by bats, often at critical stages in their annual cycle, and therefore may have an important conservation role.[31]

A commercial product marketed as "bat bark" is another promising way to provide roosting sites in places where older trees are scarce. Developed during the mid-1990s, bat bark is made from polyurethane foam and is placed on trees, where it resembles the real thing. According to Dan Garcia, a biologist in Arizona,

> What's neat is that with Bat Bark, you don't need a snag [in the tree trunk] to have the proper characteristics for a bat roost. And while loose bark on a snag may last only four to seven years, Bat Bark may have a life span of 30 to 50 years.[32]

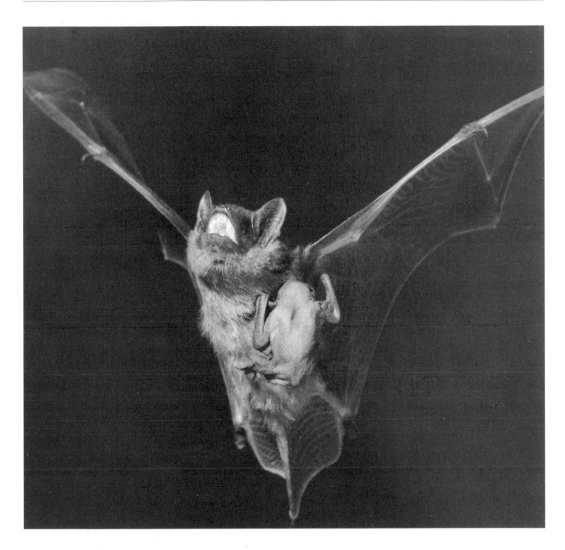

Humans have also made artificial caves designed to attract colonies of bats. In 1999 the largest artificial bat cave ever built was completed at a cost of about $250,000. Conservationist David Bamberger, who built the cave in a canyon in Johnson City, Texas, hopes it will attract a million Mexican free-tailed bats. As of spring 1999, about twenty bats had taken residence.

A mother bat carrying her young flies off into the night.

Why save bats?

Bat conservationists like to point out that bat survival is good for the earth and all living things. Like bats, humans

Bats in America's National Parks

Many national parks are helping to save bats and their habitats and are educating the public through written materials, tours, and exhibits. They have also conducted bat surveys and have erected bat gates on caves and mines to protect the animals. In addition, rangers talk about bats during evening campfire programs.

Researchers at Yosemite National Park in California have been studying the park's bats, including two species of cliff dwellers that may be endangered: western mastiff bats and spotted bats. During the 1990s researchers decided to investigate bat diversity formally, something that had not been done since 1920. Park ranger Jeffery G. Lahr worked with a team headed by Elizabeth "Dixie" Pierson and William Rainey. The team used nets to catch and observe bats flying near a river in the Wawona section of the park. During the night the researchers carefully examined various kinds of bats of different ages, including nursing females. In his 1994 article "The Bat Hunt," which appeared in the *Yosemite National Park Notebook*, Lahr wrote,

> The newly gained information on bats will be helpful in determining appropriate park management strategies. Construction of bridges (an important roosting site for bats) can be designed to provide bat roosting space. Further investigation is needed of abandoned mines around the Park and the role they play. . . . The Mastiff and the Spotted bat (both rare species) are believed to roost and forage in popular recreational use areas (rock faces and meadows). Recreational impact on these sites warrants further study. . . . During future campfires I will never look at bats in the same way. Bats will be considered honored guests, not campfire competitors. . . . Knowledge brings respect.

and animals also benefit from clean air and water and a safe food supply. Furthermore, bats are a "keystone species," meaning they propagate vegetation, thus helping other animals. Without bats, other species of plants and animals also die out or become endangered.

Bats play a vital role in maintaining the rain forest, which is essential to all life on the earth. The tropical rain forest converts carbon dioxide in the earth's atmosphere into oxygen, and the loss of trees leads to a buildup of carbon dioxide around the planet. This, in turn, lets more heat from the sun enter the earth's atmosphere but does not let enough heat leave. Trapped heat causes what scientists call the greenhouse effect and could eventually melt the polar ice caps, resulting in flooding and other problems.

In addition, numerous products and medicines come from the rain forest. New uses remain to be found for the plants that have not yet been studied.

One researcher points out the ways in which continuing bat research may inform humans:

> These diminutive creatures use highly sophisticated sonar equipment; they live for an unusually long time; and they possess virtually transparent wing membranes. Thus they are much sought for research, having contributed to navigational aids for blind people, to studies of aging processes, to development of vaccines, to testing of drugs, and to studies of creatures in space.[33]

Research with ghost bats has yielded information that is being used to develop better hearing aids. Investigators at the University of Queensland's Center for Vision, Touch, and Hearing report that the ghost bat has a unique hearing ability and can detect sounds four hundred times less intense than those heard by the human ear.

Some people say biodiversity is an important goal in itself. They contend that we do not fully understand all of the roles that different species play in the world. If species die out, there will be no chance to find out.

Altringham makes his case this way: "Why conserve bats? . . . First and foremost . . . because they have a right to a place on this planet. Bats are part of the global ecosystem, with a part to play in its survival and evolution."[34]

Appendix

Bats in Jeopardy

Extinct Bats
brown flying fox (probably)
dark flying fox
Guam flying fox (probably)
lesser yellow house bat (probably)
Negros naked-backed fruit bat (probably)
Nendo tube-nosed bat (probably)
New Zealand greater short-tailed bat
Palau flying fox
Panay giant fruit bat
Tanzanian woolly bat (probably)

Endangered Bats
Bougainville monkey-faced bat
Bulmer's fruit bat
bumblebee bat
cave myotis
Chuuk flying fox
Comoro black flying fox
cusp-toothed flying fox
Fijian monkey-faced bat
flat-headed myotis
golden bats of Mauritius Islands
golden-capped fruit bat
gray bat
grey-headed bat (Australia)
Guadalcanal monkey-faced bat
Guatemalan myotis
hairless bat
Hawaiian hoary bat

hog-nosed bat
Indiana bat
lesser bat
little Mariana fruit bat
Mariana fruit bat
Mexican long-nosed
Miller's myotis
Mortlock Islands flying fox
Ozark big-eared bat
Pemba flying fox
Philippine tube-nosed fruit bat
Pohnpei flying fox
Rafinesque's big-eared bat
Rodrigues fruit bat
Ryukyu flying fox
Seychelles sheath-tailed bat
Singapore roundleaf horseshoe bat
Virginia big-eared bat
western mastiff bat
Wroughton's free-tailed bat

Notes

Chapter 1: Helpful Flying Mammals

1. Quoted in Derek Grzelewski, "Batty About Flying Foxes," *Smithsonian,* May 2000, p. 104.

2. Alvin Novick and Bruce Dale, "Bats Aren't All Bad," *National Geographic*, May 1973, p. 616.

3. Merlin D. Tuttle, *America's Neighborhood Bats*, rev. ed. Austin: University of Texas Press, 1998, p. 14.

4. Tuttle, *America's Neighborhood Bats*, p. 15.

5. Quoted in Jeffrey P. Cohn, "Applauding the Beleaguered Bat," *Americas*, November-December 1987, p. 16.

6. Tuttle, *America's Neighborhood Bats*, p. 16.

Chapter 2: Enemies

7. Merlin D. Tuttle, "The Amazing Frog-Eating Bat," *National Geographic*, January 1982, p. 90.

8. M. Brock Fenton, *Bats*. New York: Facts On File, 1992, p. 171.

9. Grzelewski, "Batty About Flying Foxes," p. 102.

10. Quoted in Lee Wohlfert, "On the Job," *People Weekly*, October 14, 1986, p. 118.

11. Merlin D. Tuttle, "How North America's Bats Survive the Winter," *Bats*, vol. 9, no. 3, 1991.

Chapter 3: Loss of Habitats and Roosts

12. Quoted in Dana Warn, "Ancient Bat Clues: Fossil Study May Help Restore Bat Home," August 8, 2000. www.abc news.go.com/sections/science/DailyNews/bat_fossils_000807. html.

13. *Bats Magazine*, "The Fight for Mt. Etna," Summer 1989, p. 3.

Chapter 4: Rescue Efforts

14. Thomas H. Kunz and Paul A. Racey, *Bat Biology and Conservation.* Washington, DC: Smithsonian Institution Press, 1998, p. 257.

15. U.S. Fish and Wildlife Service, The Endangered Species Act of 1973, May 12, 2000. http://endangered.fws.gov/esa.html.

16. Quoted in Nicholas Payne, "Fruit Bat Off the Menu?" *Bats Magazine*, February 1984, p. 1.

17. Quoted in Morgan Simmons, "Group Works to Save Endangered Bats in Cave," *Birmingham Post-Herald*, July 21, 2000. www.postherald.com/nw072100.html.

18. Quoted in Simmons, "Group Works to Save Endangered Bats in Cave."

19. Quoted in Grzewelski, "Batty About Flying Foxes," p. 104.

20. Quoted in Nina Fascione, "The Evolving Role of American Zoos in Bat Conservation," *Bats Magazine*, Spring 1996, pp. 8–9.

Chapter 5: What Lies Ahead?

21. M. Brock Fenton, *The Bat: Wings in the Night Sky.* Buffalo, NY: Firefly Books, 1998, p. 114.

22. Luis F. Aguirre, "106 Species and Counting: Bat Conservation Comes to Bolivia," *Bats Magazine*, Winter 1998, p. 4.

23. John D. Altringham, *Bats: Biology and Behavior.* New York: Oxford University Press, 1996, p. 232.

24. Quoted in Kunz and Racey, *Bat Biology and Conservation*, p. 282.

25. Quoted in Kunz and Racey, *Bat Biology and Conservation*, p. 289.

26. Aguirre, "106 Species and Counting," p. 3.

27. Quoted in Don Hopey, "Endangered Bat Imperils Logging in National Forest," *Pittsburgh Post-Gazette*, November 19, 1998. www.post-gazette.com/healthscience/19981119bats3.asp.

28. Altringham, *Bats*, p. 232.

29. Quoted in Grzelewski, "Batty About Flying Foxes," p. 104.

30. Merlin D. Tuttle and Jim Kennedy, "Indiana Bat Hibernation Roost Evaluation," North American Bat Conservation Partnership. www.batcon.org/nabcp/newsite/accomp-ind.html.

31. John D. Altringham, "Bat Houses in British Forests," *Bats Magazine*, Spring 1998, pp. 8–11.

32. Quoted in Laurali Noteman, "Hidden Housing: Artificial Bark for Bats," *Bats Magazine*, Fall 1998, p. 13.

33. Norman J. Myers, *The Primary Source: Tropical Forests and Our Future*. New York: Norton, 1992, p. 98.

34. Altringham, *Bats*, p. 232.

Glossary

biodiversity: The variety of organisms found within a particular geographic area.

CITES: The Convention on International Trade in Endangered Species of Wild Fauna and Flora is a regulatory group that sets international trade policies involving endangered species.

echolocation: A natural form of sonar that bats use to find food and to avoid collisions in the dark. They emit high-pitched squeaking sounds that bounce off the objects around them.

ecosystem: A natural system in which various organisms function together in their environment.

endangered: A label given to a plant or animal species that is near extinction.

extinction: The complete and permanent disappearance of a species.

forage: To search an area for food or prey.

guano: Bat excrement that is often used for fertilizer.

habitat: The natural living space of a plant or animal.

hibernate: To spend the winter in an inactive or sleeping state.

humane eviction: To remove a wild animal from a home or other setting in such a way that it can survive.

insectivorous: Depending on insects for food.

keystone species: A species that is vital to the survival of an ecosystem.

nocturnal: Active after dark rather than during the daytime.

predation: The capturing of prey as a means of obtaining food for survival.

roost: A place, such as a tree, where bats rest, sleep, or stop to eat their food.

threatened: A label given to a species that is likely to become endangered if threats to its survival are not removed within the near future.

Organizations
to Contact

Bat Conservation International (BCI)
PO Box 162603
Austin, TX 78716
(512) 327-9721
website: www.batcon.org/home/index.html

The largest organization devoted to bat research, education, and conservation. BCI conducts programs throughout the world, works with many other conservation organizations, and publishes magazines and other materials about bats.

The Bat Conservation Trust (BCT)
15 Cloisters House, 8 Battersea Park Road
London SW4 4BG
England
0171 627 2629

BCT is the only organization in the United Kingdom devoted solely to conserving bats and their habitats. BCT carries out conservation projects, research, and educational activities.

Bats Northwest
PO Box 19558
Seattle, WA 98109
(206) 256-0406
website: www.batsnorthwest.org/

This nonprofit organization works to conserve bats and their habitats in the Pacific Northwest.

California Bat Conservation Fund
3053 Fillmore St. #239

San Francisco, CA 94123
(831) 426-5304
website: www.californiabats.com

This nonprofit organization works to preserve bats through educational presentations, rehabilitating injured and orphaned bats, and working with other bat conservationists.

Norfolk Bat Group
c/o John Goldsmith
Castle Museum
Norwich NR1 3JU
England
website: www.norfolk-bat-group.org.uk

The Norfolk Bat Group studies bats in England's Norfolk County, works to educate the public about bats, and provides practical assistance to groups and individuals working to conserve bats.

Organization for Bat Conservation (OBC)
1553 Haslett Rd.
Haslett, MI 48840
(517) 339-5200
website: www.batconservation.org/

The OBC is a nonprofit organization that aims to preserve bats and their habitats through education, collaboration, and research.

Urban Wildlife Rescue, Inc.
PO Box 201311
Denver, CO 80220
(303) 340-4911
Fax: (303) 363-8628
website: www.urbanwildliferescue.org/

This organization provides educational programs and helps people to humanely evict bats from their homes and businesses.

U.S. Fish and Wildlife Service
Division of Endangered Species
Mail Stop 420 ARLSQ
1849 C St. NW

Washington, DC 20240
(202) 208-4717
website: http://endangered.fws.gov/

This government organization is mandated to enforce the Endangered Species Act as well as protect plants and animals threatened with extinction. It conducts numerous educational programs in addition to monitoring wildlife and carrying out conservation efforts.

World Wildlife Fund International (WWF)

Ave du Mont-Blanc
CH 1196 Gland
Switzerland
website: www.worldwildlifefund.com

The WWF defines its mission as "to stop and hopefully reverse the accelerating degradation of the natural environment."

Suggestions for Further Reading

Books

Diane Ackerman, *Bats: Shadows in the Night*. New York: Crown, 1997. For young readers. The author describes her experiences capturing and studying bats at Big Bend National Park with bat expert Merlin D. Tuttle, whose photos illustrate the book.

M. Brock Fenton, *The Bat: Wings in the Night Sky*. Buffalo, NY: Firefly Books, 1998. A readable book with numerous color photos and basic information about bats as well as this Canadian author's personal experiences with bats around the world. Final chapters deal with conservation efforts and ongoing research.

Norman J. Myers, *The Primary Source: Tropical Forests and Our Future*. New York: Norton, 1992. A detailed look at the way tropical forests affect the global ecology and the various problems that occur with deforestation.

Klaus Richarz, *The World of Bats: The Flying Goblins of the Night*. London: TFH Publications, 1993. A comprehensive look at bats, mainly those species found in Europe; in-depth but readable, with colorful photos.

Merlin D. Tuttle, *America's Neighborhood Bats*. Rev. ed. Austin: University of Texas Press, 1998. An introduction to various bats found in America; discusses conservation, public health issues, and the bat's role in ecology. It also includes full-color photographs by the author.

Merlin D. Tuttle and D. L. Hensley, *Bat House Builder's Handbook*. Austin: Bat Conservation International, 1993. A how-to manual designed to help people design, install, and monitor bat houses that provide artificial roosting places.

D. E. Wilson, *Bats in Question: The Smithsonian Answer Book*. Washington, DC: Smithsonian Institution Press, 1997. A readable introduction to bat biology and behavior using a question-answer format. Includes material about bat conservation and photos by Merlin D. Tuttle.

Periodicals

Derek Grzelewski, "Batty About Flying Foxes," *Smithsonian,* May 2000. Numerous color photos supplement this account of Australian conservationists' efforts on behalf of beleaguered fruit bats.

Works Consulted

Books

John D. Altringham, *Bats: Biology and Behavior*. New York: Oxford University Press, 1996. Provides scientific information covering topics such as physical features, roosting habits, behavior, and conservation and is written by a respected bat scientist.

M. Brock Fenton, *Bats*. New York: Facts On File, 1992. A thorough and absorbing introduction to the physiology and behavior of bats. Includes chapters on various species, echolocation, feeding and roosting habits, and conservation issues as well as full-color illustrations.

A. M. Hutson, *Action Plan for the Conservation of Bats in the United Kingdom*. London: Bat Conservation Trust, 1993. Describes a detailed plan, including laws, designed to save endangered bats in the United Kingdom through collaboration of government and various conservation groups.

Thomas H. Kunz and Paul A. Racey, *Bat Biology and Conservation*. Washington, DC: Smithsonian Institution Press, 1998. An extensive collection of recent scientific studies on bats and conservation efforts in different regions throughout the world.

Periodicals

Luis F. Aguirre, "106 Species and Counting: Bat Conservation Comes to Bolivia," *Bats Magazine*, Winter 1998.

John D. Altringham, "Bat Houses in British Forests," *Bats Magazine,* Spring 1998.

Bats Magazine, "The Fight for Mt. Etna," Summer 1989.

————, "Long-Nosed Bats Proposed for Endangered Status," Summer 1988.

————, "What Is Your Favorite Park Doing for Bats?" Spring 1995.

Daniel Bennett et al., "Bats and Monitor Lizards on the Islands of Negros and Panay, Philippines: The Final Report of the University of Aberdeen Expedition to the Western Visayas, Philippines," Aberdeen, Scotland: Viper Press, 1997.

Jeffrey P. Cohn, "Applauding the Beleaguered Bat," *Americas,* November-December 1987.

D. H. Cumming et al., "Elephant Impacts on Biodiversity of Miombo Woodlands in Zimbabwe," *South African Journal of Science,* vol. 93, 1997.

Mike Daniel, "New Zealand's Unique Burrowing Bats Are Endangered," *Bats Magazine,* September 1985.

Nina Fascione, "The Evolving Role of American Zoos in Bat Conservation," *Bats Magazine,* Spring 1996.

Theodore H. Fleming, "Climb Every Cactus: BCI's Sonoran Desert Bat–Cactus Project Concludes Its First Field Season in Mexico," *Bats Magazine,* Fall 1989.

Barbara French, "Where the Bats Are, Part I: Plants and Trees," *Bats Magazine,* Spring 1999.

G. Jones, P. L. Duverge, and R. D. Ransome, "Conservation Biology of an Endangered Species: Field Studies of Greater Horseshoe Bats," *Symposia of the Zoological Society of London,* vol. 67, 1995.

Kate McAney, "On the Job—Bat Conservation in Ireland," *Bats Magazine,* Summer 1998.

Laurali Noteman, "Hidden Housing: Artificial Bark for Bats," *Bats Magazine,* Fall 1998.

Alvin Novick and Bruce Dale, "Bats Aren't All Bad," *National Geographic,* May 1973.

Nicholas Payne, "Fruit Bat Off the Menu?" *Bats Magazine*, February 1984.

Carmel Schrire, "In New Guinea's Threatened Wilds," *Boston Globe*, January 24, 1999.

Anastasia Toufexis, "Bats' New Image: Researchers Say They're Benign, Useful, and Endangered," *Time*, August 21, 1995.

Merlin D. Tuttle, "The Amazing Frog-Eating Bat," *National Geographic*, January 1982.

———, "Bats—the Cactus Connection," *National Geographic*, June 1991.

———, "Gentle Flyers of the African Night," *National Geographic*, April 1986.

———, "How North America's Bats Survive the Winter," *Bats*, vol. 9, no. 3, 1991. www.batcon.org/batsmag/v9n3-2.html.

———, "Photographing the World's Bats: Adventure, Tribulation, and Rewards," *Bats Magazine*, Winter 1988.

———, "Saving North America's Beleagured Bats," *National Geographic*, February 1995.

Kim Whitman, "A Personal Portrait of the Rodrigues Fruit Bat," *Bats Magazine*, Winter 1998.

Lee Wohlfert, "On the Job," *People Weekly*, October 14, 1986.

Internet Sources

Patrick Beach, "Bracken Cave Near San Antonio," *American-Statesman,* June 14, 1998. www.austin360.com/local/bats2/brackencave.htm.

Michael A. Bogan, "Potential Effects of Global Change on Bats." http://geochange.er.usgs.gov/sw/impacts/biology/bats.

Common Dreams Newswire, "Citizen Suit Filed to Protect Habitat in Guam," April 3, 2000. www.commondreams.org/news2000/0403-08.htm.

Great Basin National Park, "Bats," December 1999. www.nps.gov/grba/bats.htm.

Don Hopey, "Endangered Bat Imperils Logging in National Forest," *Pittsburgh Post-Gazette,* November 19, 1998. www.post-gazette.com/healthscience/19981119bats3.asp.

Heidi Jamieson, "Conservation on the Island of Rodrigues, Mauritius, Indian Ocean," Bat Conservation International, www.batconservation.org/content/meetourbats/rodbatinfo.htm.

Jeffery G. Lahr, "The Bat Hunt," *Yosemite National Park Notebook*, Summer 1994. www.nps.gov/yose/notes/note4.htm.

Ministry of Environment, Lands, and Parks, Wildlife Branch, "Endangered Spotted Bats of British Columbia: Spotted Bats at Risk in British Columbia." www.cancaver. ca/bats/bc/spotdbat.htm.

Monday Paper, "Bat Action Team Rallies to Rescue Cape Bats," March 13–20, 2000. www.uct.ac.za/general/monpaper/ 2k-no05/bats.htm.

North American Bat Conservation Partnership, "The Great Lakes Region Bat Conservation Initiative." www.batcon. org/nabcp/newsite/accomp-glm.html.

Rachel Nowak, "Strange Fruit," *New Scientist*, November 21, 1998. www.newscientist.com/ns/981121/nbats.html.

Morgan Simmons, "Group Works to Save Endangered Bats in Cave," *Birmingham Post-Herald,* July 21, 2000. www.postherald. com/nw072100.html.

Cara Spindler, "A Few Hard Facts About Bats: Not So Bad After All," *University Record,* March 8, 1999. www.umich. edu/~urecord/9899/Mar08_99/bats.htm.

Merlin D. Tuttle and Jim Kennedy, "Indiana Bat Hibernation Roost Evaluation," North American Bat Conservation Partnership. www.batcon.org/nabcp/newsite/accomp-ind.html.

Urban Wildlife Rescue, Inc., "Pombo the Bat." www.urban wildliferescue.org/rescues/pombo.

U.S. Fish and Wildlife Service, Division of Endangered Species, "Common Misconceptions About Bats." http://endangered.fws.gov/bats/miscon.htm.

U.S. Fish and Wildlife Service, The Endangered Species Act of 1973, May 12, 2000. http://endangered.fws.gov/esa.html.

————, "Reasons for Decline." http://endangered.fws.gov/bats/threats.htm.

————, "Threatened and Endangered Species: Mariana Fruit Bats/Fanihi." http://pacificislands.fws.gov/wesa/marianabatindex.html.

Dana Warn, "Ancient Bat Clues: Fossil Study May Help Restore Bat Home," August 8, 2000. www.abcnews.go.com/sections/science/DailyNews/bat_fossils_000807.html.

Wildlife Trust, "Livingstone's Fruit Bat." www.thewildones.org/Animals/livstone.html.

Index

Picture Credits

Cover photo: © Merlin D. Tuttle/Bat Conservation International

© Elaine Acker/Bat Conservation International, 69

Archive Photos, 13

© Gary Braasch/Corbis, 27

Lynwood Chace/Archive Photos, 87

© Corbis, 10, 59

Digital Vision, Environmental Issues, 42

© Gregory G. Dimijian, 1995/Photo Researchers, Inc., 38

©Stephen Dalton/Photo Researchers, Inc., 54

Michael Durham/gerryellis.com, 55

© Owen Franken/Corbis, 39

© Frederica Georgia/Photo Researchers, Inc., 82

© Woodrow Goodpaster/National Audubon Society/Photo Researchers, Inc., 47

Hulton Getty/Archive Photos, 15

© Peter Johnson/Corbis, 52

© Mark Kisser/Bat Conservation International, 99

© Lake County Museum/Corbis, 63

© Frederick McKinney, 1997/FPG International, 45

© Sally A. Morgan, Ecoscene/Corbis, 29

PhotoDisk, Vol. 44, Nature, Wildlife and the Environment, 88, 91, 93

Photo Researchers, Inc., 101

© Joel W. Rogers/Corbis, 57

Martha Schierholz, 18, 33, 98

© Telegraph Colour Library, 1997/FPG International, 51

© Merlin Tuttle/Bat Conservation International, 7, 16, 19, 20, 23, 25, 26, 34, 44, 64, 77, 79

© Merlin D. Tuttle/Bat Conservation International/Photo Researchers, Inc., 35, 71, 75

© Merlin Tuttle/Photo Researchers, Inc., 22

© VCG, 1999/FPG International, 61

© Dr. Paul A. Zahl/Photo Researchers, Inc., 94

About the Author

Victoria Sherrow holds B.S. and M.S. degrees from Ohio State University. Among her writing credits are numerous stories and articles, ten books of fiction, and more than fifty books of nonfiction for children and young adults. Her recent books have explored such topics as biomedical ethics, the Great Depression, and the Holocaust. For Lucent Books, she has written *The Titanic, Life During the Gold Rush,* and *The Righteous Gentiles.* Sherrow lives in Connecticut with her husband, Peter Karoczkai, and their three children.